CHOOSING HAPPIER

HOW TO BE HAPPY
despite your circumstances, history or genes

BY JEM FRIAR

The Practical Happiness Series

(Book 1)

IMAGINAL
PUBLISHING

Published by Imaginal Publishing

Cover design by: Predrag Čapo

Print Book ISBN: 978-0-9956811-2-5
E-book ISBN: 978-0-9956811-1-8

Typeset in Cambria and Wingdings with permission from Microsoft.

FREE HAPPINESS TOOLKIT

To support you in your desire to be happier I have created several tools and resources for you to download. These include printable tracking sheets, reminder cards, pay it forwards cards, MP3 meditations, etc. They will make your journey to increasing happiness easier, more effective, fun and enjoyable and they are all FREE.

Don't wait until you finish reading the book to get them, as they will be very helpful to have from the start. These tools will make it simpler for you to apply many of the practical exercises that are within this book and they are essential if you truly want to make a lasting change.

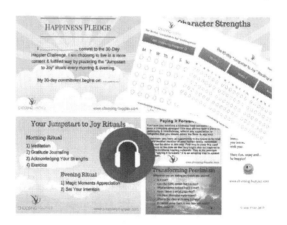

I have also created the "My Happiness Journal" which is a workbook that has been designed to be used in conjunction with this book. As you already have this Choosing Happier book, you will get a 30% off discount code for the journal that will be sent to you with the resources in the Happiness Toolkit.

I will be creating even more useful aids to support you in living a more joy-full life and will inform you in the future as and when this toolbox increases! To access these tools and to get your discount code, just follow the link below.

To get access to your Free Happiness Toolkit go to

http://www.choosing-happier.com/reader-bonuses

AUDIOBOOK

Would you like to listen to Choosing Happier wherever you go? This book should soon be available as an audiobook (in fact, by the time that you read this it may already be). If you would like to get this book in its downloadable recorded form, please go to this page

http://www.choosing-happier.com/happiness-audiobook

It will be possible to buy the book on iTunes, Audible and Amazon shortly but **you may be able to get it for free** too. So please go to the link above first to find out.

PUBLISHER'S NOTES

Disclaimer

This publication is intended to provide helpful and informative material. It is not intended to diagnose, treat, cure, or prevent any health problem or condition, nor is it intended to replace the advice of a physician. No action should be taken solely on the contents of this book. Always consult your physician or qualified healthcare professional on any matters regarding your health and before adopting any suggestions in this book or drawing inferences from it.

The author and publisher specifically disclaim all responsibility for any liability, loss or risk, personal or otherwise, which is incurred as a consequence, directly or indirectly, from the use or application of any contents of this book.

Any and all product names referenced within this book are the trademarks of their respective owners. None of these owners have sponsored, authorized, endorsed, or approved this book.

(Should you practice any of the exercises presented in this book there is a very high likelihood that you may well end up more content in life and smiling a lot, which can be disconcerting for those who have not yet learnt how to be happier. In such cases, it is recommended that you encourage other people to read this book so that they can also raise their happiness levels and feel at ease with your new levels of joy.)

Kindle Edition 2016

Manufactured in the United States of America

DEDICATION

This book is dedicated to the creation of a happier, kinder, more balanced and peaceful humanity on this beautiful planet.

"Happiness is not something you postpone for the future; it is something you design for the present."
– Jim Rohn

"Happiness is when what you think, what you say, and what you do are in harmony."
– Mahatma Gandhi

"The most important thing is to enjoy your life—to be happy—it's all that matters."
— Audrey Hepburn

THE HAPPIER PLANET MISSION STATEMENT

To inspire and enable people to live more content and happy lives so that we all express and experience a greater level of kindness, care and consciousness. In this way, humanity as a whole will be able to thrive in an environmentally sustainable, benevolent, socially just and peaceful way on planet Earth.

"My commitment is to help support positive change on this planet – one heart smile at a time."
– Jem Friar

WHY YOU SHOULD READ THIS BOOK

"Happiness doesn't depend on who you are or what you have, it depends solely on what you think." – Dale Carnegie

There is a general belief held by many people that we cannot choose how happy we are, that our happiness is a result of our genes, our brain chemistry, our history, our family, our circumstances and even just down to our luck. I have written this book to show you that this is not true. In actual fact, anyone can change their levels of happiness by consciously changing their mindset and their habits. My aim is to help you to do just that.

There are three great motivators in life that impel us to act, think or speak in any given circumstance. These are:

1) **Survival** – to meet our needs for food, water, connection and shelter (and procreation when we take into account the biologically imperative of our species too.)

2) **Pleasure** or the experience of good feelings.

3) **Pain** or the avoidance of bad/uncomfortable feelings.

This book is focused on the second great motivator – increasing the amount of good or positive feelings that we experience. It is, after all, so often the driving force behind so many of the things that we do and pursue. Unfortunately, many of the ways that we attempt to find increased happiness are often ineffective or unsustainable. By this, I mean that we try to become happier by means that do not actually work, certainly not for an extended period. They may also be harmful to us and/or the people and the world around us. With this in mind, it would seem very sensible just to cut to the chase and discover what can effectively enable us to experience more positive emotions in an ongoing and sustainable way.

The skills that you will develop by reading this book will also have a very useful impact on the third great motivator – your desire to avoid pain! As you become increasingly positive and optimistic, you will be less likely to get caught in negative emotions, whilst being more resilient and able to move through challenges.

Fascinatingly, becoming happier makes us more effective at meeting our survival needs too. Happier people are more effective, productive and healthy, as well as better at developing good social connections and relationships!

Before I go any further, let me just clarify what I mean by happiness. The intention of this book is not to make you happy, happy, happy all of the time, as a way to avoid difficult emotions or to impress other people. This would be taking us into the realms of the potentially frivolous, self-serving and ungrounded pursuit of a form of happiness which is inauthentic, unnatural and potentially destructive! Rather, my intention is to enable you to experience more positive states on a day to day basis and be increasingly at ease and content. It is about developing the skills that will nourish you on a deep level and allow you to enjoy and appreciate life much more.

Nearly everyone wants to be happy but when it comes down to it most people are not very clear about how to actually become happier. Most people think that happiness will come in the future when something happens – a job, a raise, a relationship, some good fortune, etc. We constantly pursue various things in the hope that they will bring us happiness but these things do not guarantee that we will become happier at all and certainly not on a long-lasting basis.

If being happy were just about what we owned and earned, as we are so often told by the advertising industry, then we should be quite ecstatic at this point. However, in the past forty years, although the average income in the USA has tripled, happiness levels have hardly changed and are, in fact, slightly lower than they were. At the same time, depression has rapidly increased (1 in 2 people in the Western world are now likely to suffer from depression.) Why, when we have so much, are we not satisfied?

Our general levels of discontent seem to have increased recently for several reasons. Many of our beliefs about how to be happy are false. Our consumer society conditioning has had a massive negative impact by keeping us focused on where we are lacking. Unnatural modern-day ways of living in regards to having fewer real social connections, poor diet and exercise habits affect our capacity to be happy as well.

These are some of our contemporary challenges but we also have to look at an obstacle that humanity has always had to overcome when attempting to find contentment and joy; for we are confronted by a more biological hurdle – our brains have a natural negativity bias. This is an evolutionary trait that helped our ancestors to survive by ena-bling them to constantly be aware of potential threats and danger. However, in our modern relatively safe environment it is wise to learn how to consciously override this trait if you wish to maintain higher levels of optimism and positivity.

We will explore the main reasons why we are not as happy as we could be at the start of the book because understanding what you are up against will make moving beyond it all the easier. From there, I will guide you through many questions, practices, and exercises that will help you to perceive and act in life in much more positive ways and thus enable you to raise your basic happiness level.

Reading this book will help you to experience more positive emotions and be more resilient in the face of challenges in life – if you practice the suggested exercises and if you are willing to explore perceiving your world in different ways!

If that last sentence made you panic or shrink inside, don't worry be-cause any exercises that I suggest in this book are easy and quick to do. What is more, they are enjoyable and will inspire good feelings, which in turn makes them even more undemanding.

Increasing your positivity is a great goal to have in life yet it has been shown in countless research findings that being happier leads to various other brilliant consequences too because **happiness is an enabler**.

When people are happier they were found to:

✓ be more successful in their work
✓ be more productive
✓ be more creative
✓ have more energy
✓ have better health
✓ recover more quickly from illness
✓ enjoy life's everyday experiences more
✓ be more resilient when faced with difficult situations
✓ have stronger friendships and better social networks
✓ have healthier and happier relationships.

So if any of these outcomes are at all appealing to you as well as the idea of being generally happier then this book will be extremely useful for you.

Beyond this, there are three things that you really need to know:

1) Happiness is a choice. This book will help you to really understand this fact and to inspire you to make that choice more easily.

2) Happiness is a skill and a practice that can be learned. With the right practices and mindset, it becomes straightforward to raise your daily happiness levels.

3) It is solely up to you to make choosing and being happy a major priority in your life – no one else will or can do it for you! Hoping that other people or things will make you happy is ineffective and disempowering.

The good news is that with the information in this book you can now make this choice much more easily and effectively. It will provide you with the tools, practices, habits, and ways of perceiving that will offer a lasting and practical answer to the "how to be happy" question.

With that clarified, I encourage you to dive straight into this exciting, inspiring and uplifting journey into the wisdom of happiness and joy. Read on, dear fellow traveler...

WHY I WROTE THIS BOOK

In many ways, I was lucky to grow up in London, England in the 1970s. Kids in our neighborhood played outside together in the streets and parks, television was good quality but limited (there were only three channels to choose from and even then, only at certain times of the day), our family felt stable and my mum was a great cook. My father, John, was a very humorous and kind man who definitely had a big influence on the development of my humor and perspective on life.

At school, my joking and mischievous pranks earned me good standing amongst my peers, whilst at the same time, no doubt caused regular frustration for my teachers. The habit of looking for the funny sides of situations also helped me, to a degree, to get through some of the tough experiences of growing up. Little did I know it, but I had already developed and obtained two of the benefits of being happy – better social connections and greater resilience.

My interest and fascination with our capacity to be happy (despite our circumstance) began in my twenties when I spent a decade traveling and working my way around the world. Something that I observed was that many people that I met who lived in basic or challenging conditions seemed to be much happier than many affluent people that I knew in the modern Western world. Having been conditioned to believe that happiness correlated to how secure your world was and how much you owned, this observation seemed to be a bizarre paradox.

I also noticed that some cultures and countries just seemed to be happier than others and this appeared to be based on their perception of life and reality i.e. their thoughts, beliefs and ways of living were more conducive to enjoying life and being happier in the moment.

I believe that if one person (or whole culture) can live in a certain way, then it is possible for others to learn to live in that way too. To that end, I often found myself attempting to understand and deconstruct the values and perspectives that were foundational for those happier cultures and people, with the intention of adopting them myself.

I am fascinated about anything to do with the conscious practice of self-development and personal growth. Our ability to learn new ways of being and thinking and our capacity to let go of habits, beliefs and thought patterns that do not serve our highest good in exchange for ones that do, are invaluable skills to learn that can deeply support our growth and evolution.

I made a commitment to continuously attempt to grow and learn many years ago and have done my best to keep it. For me, this has been by embracing the lessons in life that come my way, learning from others and gaining knowledge from experiences workshops, books and courses that were designed to inspire personal development and discovery. I have also explored my spiritual side through meditation, vision quests, and other inner initiatory experiences and retreats. They have all brought me to where I am in this moment and I am truly grateful for them. I am also happier because of it, as one of the keys to becoming happier is fulfilling our need to have a sense of ongoing self-growth and learning.

Embracing positive change has been important for me outside of my own journey too. In my work coaching or facilitating retreats and workshops, I am keen to help others find balance, grow and make positive shifts. I am enthusiastic about supporting such transformations in others because change has been so valuable for me. It is also incredibly rewarding to do work where I get to witness people drop their old emotional baggage, flourish, reconnect with themselves and generally become happier and healthier.

One thing that I have observed in my work and in my experience is that *behind all the imbalances and struggles, the learning, the inner journeying, the trauma, the dropping of negative beliefs, the desire for change and a better life there lies a basic and simple longing for happiness in everyone.*

A couple of years ago I turned my full attention to what could be called the science of happiness – positive psychology. This is a new and inspiring branch of psychology that was only born in the 1990s. Positive psychology studies what enables people to be happy, positive, in the flow and successful. It is full of invaluable tools and practices that enable anyone to increase their level of happiness and positive emotions.

I quickly became hooked on learning about positive psychology because it resonated with many of my own conclusions about life and our potential to change how we live to a much more joy-filled way of being. Rather than just study this fascinating subject, I decided to practice the techniques that I was learning on a daily basis to see how effective they were for me before I began suggesting them to my clients.

Like everyone, I have gone through various emotional roller coaster rides and challenges in life. I have felt hopeless, depressed, disheartened and even despair about certain situations in my darkest times. It is our nature as human beings to live through an immense range of feelings in response to our experience of life. However, on the whole, I had previously perceived myself as a fairly balanced, happy and healthy individual, so the shifts that I have experienced have quite surprised me. Just by committing to a few simple daily practices, I have found that my positivity, contentedness, centeredness, kindness and personal resilience have all improved remarkably!

Inspired by my own experience, I have been encouraging my coaching clients to integrate these exercises and understandings into their lives and they have also reported great successes. It is precisely because these practices have proved themselves to be so effective that I decided to put them in an easy to understand and practical form so that they will be accessible to more people i.e. this book.

Reaching and inspiring as many people as possible with this information is important to me for five reasons.

Firstly, I have a sense of humanity as a whole living in a very out of balance and unsustainable way at present. Like lemmings who think that they are rushing off for a day at the beach, this doesn't look good from an objective viewpoint.

We are oblivious to how our consumerism and individualism is having a massive negative effect around the planet, both on the ecosystems and environment, and on other members of our human family. For most of our existence, humans have only been a tiny part of the biosphere of the Earth, with limited capabilities and thus have had minimal impact upon it. However, that has radically changed because there are now 7.5 billion of us and we have the capacity to wield a multitude of ecosystem shattering technologies. It is, therefore, imperative that we evolve our ways of thinking to be more global, wise and consciously benevolent.

Secondly, I believe that developing the ability to be more content, happy and caring, will motivate and enable people to effectively make positive changes and live in a balanced and harmonious way. Two of the most powerful ways of raising our personal happiness are by practicing gratitude (which helps us to recognize how much we already have and so be less likely to constantly crave more) and being kind and generous to others. These practices encourage us to shift to a more global and caring perspective – something that I believe is imperative if humanity is going to evolve into the benign, peaceful and conscious presence that it needs to be.

Thirdly, I have worked with many people who have been unnecessarily stuck in states of depression and negativity for years. Often, the only options that people in these incapacitating states are given or can find are suppressive pharmaceutical drugs, self-chosen addictions or the discouraging belief that it is all because of their brain chemistry, history or genes.

Yet, I have seen how it is possible for people to shift out of such debilitating emotions and thought patterns just by learning some simple new habits and ways of perceiving and relating to themselves and their reality. It seems a tragedy that so many people are normally left in such a disempowered and hopeless position when there are viable and effective alternatives.

The practices presented in this book can be potent antidotes to stuck negativity, so it is my hope that many people will find that adopting them as regular habits will enable a shift in their states and change their lives in a very empowering way. I have provided a lot of exercises in the book, extra support materials, and an ongoing community to help make this transformation easier.

Fourthly, the more people who become skilled at living more happily, the more people they will impact and inspire to also be happier. Happiness escalates, so the effects of this book will multiply far beyond just those who read it.

Finally, when we are happier we are more productive, creative, successful and healthy. If we are to make big changes in the way that we are living on the planet, then it would be great to do it as creatively, proficiently, efficiently, and successfully as possible, whilst being healthy and enjoying the process.

N.B. My goal in writing this book was not about providing you with some interesting ideas or concepts for you to think about and then forget when you move on to your next book. Rather, this book is full of potent questions for you to answer and practical exercises for you to do. In this way, you can start to experience greater levels of contentment, happiness, and joy in your life right now.

My purpose behind this book is to facilitate your positive transformation. All of the tools to enable this are found in the following chapters – you just need to commit to contemplating and responding to the questions and to doing the practices.

To make your journey into greater happiness and fulfillment even easier I have also created many extra tools to help you that include:

- The free Happiness Toolkit (this includes Paying it Forwards cards, a 30 Day Happiness Exercise Record Sheet to keep your momentum rolling, a Happier Pledge to inspire your commitment, guided MP3 meditations, etc.)

- The *Jumpstart to Joy* morning ritual to make sure that you get out on the right side of the bed (the happy side), every day of your life!

- The *My Happiness Journal* to make doing the exercises easier.

- A private online community where you can be inspired, motivated and supported by each other.

***

A couple of years ago I made a commitment to look for ways to help make massive positive change happen on this planet. Spreading these ideas and practices through writing this book and creating the www.choosing-happier.com website are part of that promise.

– Jem Friar (Feb 2016)

How To Read This Book

The book has been written in four parts. The first section gives an overview of happiness and why we are not as happy as we could be. The second section provides a selection of some of the most effective practices for becoming happier. The third section looks at attitudes, perspectives, and ways of being that make it much easier to live in a happy and balanced way. The fourth section is an inspiring look at how being happier impacts the world around us as well as the potential for scaling up happier living to groups, communities, and even countries.

Throughout the second and third sections of the book, you will find various exercises which can be identified by being in grey text boxes.

When you reach Part 2 of the book I encourage you to start doing at least one or two of these practices regularly even as you continue to read the book. It can be very helpful to get a journal specifically for this purpose. (I have designed the "My Happiness Journal" that can make doing this much easier with many of the exercises in this book included in it. You will find links to it later on.) It is, of course, most valuable to experiment with and try all the suggested exercises over time. Keep doing the ones that you enjoy and find most helpful. These are amazing keys to enable you to become happier.

This is a practical book written to enable you to actually become happier if you try these practices and adopt these ways of being. Once you have read the whole book you can easily skim back through it to look for and repeat the exercises and practices that are **written in bold.** You could do the exercises randomly or methodically go through each of the practical chapters one at a time. As such, this book will become a very useful *Happiness Manual*.

Perhaps the most valuable chapter to enable you to integrate the exercises and wisdom contained in this book into your life is Chapter 11, *The Jumpstart to Joy*. Here you will learn a couple of very easy to adopt daily practices that can totally transform your way of being. I encourage you to take the *30 day happier challenge* and do this for a whole month so that you can clearly experience the resultant positive changes in your mood, perspective, and way of being. By doing so, you will also find that these practices have become habits that you can effortlessly continue. You could start this challenge as soon as you get to chapter 11.

One of the keys to happiness is to make space in your life to actively do things with friends. Therefore, as another option, you may find it more inspiring and easier to do the exercises with a chosen friend or "Joy Buddy" or indeed a group of friends. If you are both or all reading this book at the same time, you could feasibly dedicate one or two weeks to each of the practice chapters in turn. If you cannot easily find a joy buddy in your circle of friends then there is a private Choosing Happier online community (that you are about to be invited to) which is a great place to ask and look for joy buddies. This will make the process a lot more fun and supportive, as well as provide the opportunity for mutual feedback and the sense of being on a journey together.

Whether you go through this book on your own or you share the experience, if you embrace the concepts and exercises it will have a positive, life changing effect that will guide you to a much happier, more content and joyful way of living. So enjoy the journey...

A Special Invitation

Going it alone and trying to make positive changes on your own can be very challenging. By comparison, having the support of being connected to other like-minded people who are attempting to make similar positive shifts can make such a transition much easier, more enjoyable and quite invaluable. To this end, I have created a Facebook community page that is for readers of this book who would like such support. This FB page is a place where everyone can share their gratitudes, successes, challenges, support, inspirations, "happy dances" or random acts of kindness. It is also a place where you can find "joy buddies" to help keep you accountable to your practices and commitments to living in a happier, kinder and more generous way.

I check in personally on the page and moderate the posts to keep them on track. When I have time, I even respond directly to posts and comments, so it will be great to connect with you there.

If you would like to be part of this community and gain that mutual support, encouragement, and connection in an ongoing way, then just go over to http://www.choosing-happier.com/community and ask to become a member.

TABLE OF CONTENTS

PART 1

HAPPINESS – THE OVERVIEW

A FABLE FOR SEARCHING FOR HAPPINESS

This is a short story about Mulla Nasrudin who is a character used in the ancient Sufi mystic teachings.

᳚᳚᳚

One night, Mulla Nasrudin was seen on his hands and knees under the lamplight in the street outside his house. Concerned by this, his neighbor went over to ask what was wrong. Nasrudin looked up and said, "I am searching for my key. I have lost it."

The kindly neighbor offered to help and both of them spent the next 20 minutes crawling around in the dirt, looking under every leaf and stone.

Finally, the neighbor stood up feeling exasperated and said, "Are you sure that you lost your key here because we have looked everywhere and not found anything?"

Mulla Nasrudin looked up and replied, "No, no, I didn't lose it out here. I lost it inside the house but it is dark in there so I am looking out here under the lamplight where I can see!"

᳚᳚᳚

Most people are looking for happiness in the wrong places. Finding happiness is an inside job and this book will give you the tools to discover where and how to consistently find yours.

CHAPTER 1. UNDERSTANDING HAPPINESS

"Happiness is the meaning and the purpose of life, the whole aim and end of human existence." – Aristotle

If you want to be happier in your life or maybe you would like to understand how some people are able to maintain higher levels of happiness for more of the time, then you are reading the right book to begin that journey of discovery. You are also not alone in this quest for understanding happiness. Had you done a Google search in 2005 and typed in "how to be" the first suggestion by the Google search engine would have been "rich." However, if you had typed in that question in 2016, the first suggestion would have been "happy."

I believe that this growing desire to understand how we can actually become happier is a result of the increasingly obvious failure of the acquisition model – the idea that the more we have, the happier we will become. Even though our incomes and possessions have multiplied many times over, our happiness levels have not changed whilst our rates of depression have actually increased! It has been suggested that we are suffering from *affluenza* – the emotional distress that arises from the preoccupation with possessions and appearance. It's time to find a cure.

My goal is not to help you become constantly happy in a glib, frivolous or superficial way. Rather, it is about enabling you to maintain positive states of being which are above the levels that you are used to. It is about increasing your capacity to **choose to be happier**.

I wrote this book to inspire and enable people to become happier, right now, in their everyday lives. I did not write it to help people to become more successful or to achieve greater things (although it must be noted that happier people are statistically more likely to be successful), as there are many books and seminars on that subject already. However, I am wary of remaining focused purely on such attainment goals, because it is all too easy to use them in the pursuit of happiness without necessarily leading to actually experiencing greater happiness. Added to this, I believe that it is really important for as many of us as possible to start making positive changes in the world and just pursuing success and achievement for personal gain without heart-fullness and a sense of working and creating for the greater good is unlikely to result in such shifts.

The modern and ancient wisdom that I have distilled into this book is, in effect, a step by step guide to enable you to understand the happiness factors and to increase your capability of consciously becoming happier in an easy and enjoyable way.

My approach, whenever I learn, teach or share information, is always to simplify, clarify and make things easy to understand and try. I am a firm believer in K.I.S.S. or "Keep It Super Simple" so I have laid out this book in that way. I find that things are much easier to learn and to practically apply if kept on this level. The risk of making things complicated and over-intellectualizing them is that we can end up just collecting fascinating mental concepts or become confused. Either way, we are less likely to actually adopt and try out these understandings and as a result, they are unlikely to have any impact on our lives. They will never move from just being knowledge to becoming true wisdom.

For this book to be really useful it is incredibly important that you actually try out the different exercises within each chapter. The exercises are uncomplicated and easy to do. Many can be done in just a few minutes yet they can have a profound impact. You may not feel that you have time to practice all of them and that is fine. Pick one or two to try for a couple of weeks and see how you get on with them.

CAN WE ACTUALLY CHOOSE TO BE HAPPIER?

"The last of the great human freedoms is to be able to choose our attitude in any given circumstance." – Viktor Frankl

You may be wondering if this actually is a choice that you have in the first place. So much of our conditioning and modern education is quite disempowering and infers that you are completely limited by your genes, circumstances, and luck. However, scientists have concluded that only up to 50% of our happiness levels can be traced to genetics (and having read a lot of epigenetics and interviewed the incredibly inspiring epigeneticist Bruce Lipton Ph.D., I would actually argue that it may well be less than this), whilst 10% of our happiness levels are caused by our circumstances.

This means that a massive 40% of the causes of happiness are in our control! And by in our control, I mean that they are caused by our thought patterns and habits which can all be changed by the very simple daily practices outlined in this book.

Happiness is actually a choice. Our levels of happiness are not dependent on our genes, our brain's biochemistry, our history or our circumstances. We actually have the possibility to increase our happiness by changing our habits and our mindset. This book will provide you with the understandings and tools to do precisely that.

> *"Conditions do not control your destiny – but character does. Your character is determined by your habits."* – Derek Rydall

An exciting change of paradigm called brain plasticity or neuroplasticity happened in the 1970s. Until that point, the scientific consensus had been that our brains develop and grow only during childhood and then remain static or deteriorate after that point. The discovery of brain plasticity has since shown that our brain's thinking capacity can continually grow.

Whenever we consistently and regularly focus and practice thinking in new ways, our brains develop new neural pathways so that we literally have a greater capacity to think and to do so faster, in these new ways. As such we can develop new habits and thought patterns that become increasingly easy to maintain and use.

Most of our behaviors and ways of thinking are designed by default. We pick them up from the culture that we are born into and then further develop them out of reaction, convenience, comfort or self-preservation. By consciously choosing to learn about and practice the skills of happiness, you are taking the reins and creating your life how you actually want it to be.

THE KEY IS TO CREATE HAPPINESS HABITS

"All men are the same, except for their habits." – Confucius

The fundamental essence of making the change to a more positive state of being is the adoption of simple habits that can radically change how you perceive and act in your reality. Happier people have daily habits and ways of perceiving their world that engender that state of being. Conversely, people who are unhappy or even depressed will have habits that encourage the opposite way of being. So the trick is to find and adopt the happy habits. Luckily for you, it just so happens that these are one of the main things that I am going to reveal to you throughout this book.

PRACTICE AND USE A HAPPINESS JOURNAL

The process of adopting new happiness habits and practices is enhanced by the use of a journal specifically for this purpose. Being committed to some simple, written daily practices will have a profound effect on you, as I will explain in later chapters. Having a pleasing journal and a nice pen in an accessible place close at hand will help to make this process effortless.

If you already keep a journal, that's great – you just need to adapt how you use it slightly. If not, then you will find the "My Happiness Journal" incredibly useful. I designed it to support you to practice the core most effective principles and exercises that have been proven to elevate your mood and happiness levels on a consistent basis.

4

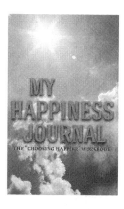

To get this Happiness Journal at a discounted price go to the Reader Bonus Materials page at the end of the book, where you will find a link to the Free Happiness Tools webpage. You will then automatically be sent a coupon code and link that will enable you to buy it directly for much less than the normal retail price.

WHAT IS THE OPPOSITE OF HAPPINESS?

"The greatest happiness is to know the source of unhappiness." – Fyodor Dostoevsky

It may seem a strange question to look at first, but to understand happiness we also need to understand what unhappiness is and its causes.

It is generally assumed that the opposite of happiness must simply be unhappiness. However, I would assert that it is much more than that and suggest that it includes living in a place of disconnection, purpose-lessness, pessimism, ingratitude, and inertia whilst often being driven by fear and insecurity. It is also reflected in the increasing levels of depression that are being experienced (50% of people in the modern Western world are now likely to suffer from depression at some point!)

As we journey through this chapter, we will also be looking at various aspects of unhappiness as a way to start to find clues as to how we can actively choose to be happier.

WHAT IS HAPPINESS TO YOU?

Before you read on I would like to ask you to take 10 minutes to do this exercise. Find a pen and a piece of paper or your journal and write down what happiness means to you.

Why do you want to be happier? What does happier look like? How would it feel? How would it change things for you if you were happier more of the time?

Keep your answers where you can easily re-read them and reflect on them. This will enable you to notice if your thoughts change as well as help you to recognize your achievement of happier states of being as they begin to become more part of your life.

HAPPINESS – A MODERN UNDERSTANDING

Much of the wisdom that I am sharing in this book is based on the many scientific research projects that have been undertaken in the disciplines of Positive Psychology and Neuroscience. Some of this wisdom has of course been known and understood for millennia but what is great about this new research is that it provides empirical data that proves how effective these techniques and habits are. In a world where we have been conditioned to only believe and trust in something once a scientist has said it is a fact, this is great news.

WHAT IS POSITIVE PSYCHOLOGY?

This was a term coined by Martin Seligman Ph.D. in the 1990s and it refers to a radical change of approach to the study and practice of psychology. Previously, psychologists had always focused their studies, research and therapy on looking at the problems, traumas, and psychoses that people suffered from. They attempted to help people who were struggling with mental issues to become "normal."

The main problem with this is that normal in our modern society is not that great and is often a long way from being optimal.

"The skills of becoming happy turn out to be almost entirely different from the skills of not being sad, not being anxious, or not being angry." – Martin Seligman

---

By contrast, positive psychologists have studied the other end of the human spectrum of experience, in search of what makes some people happier, more positive, resilient, creative, efficient and successful.

From the findings of this type of research, it has been possible to map out what people need to do to reach an optimal mental and emotional way of living. As such, positive psychology can be defined as the scientific study of optimal human functioning.

Another difference about positive psychology is that it is less focused on the medium of having a psychologist who has to work directly with an individual. Rather, it has provided lots of information and easy to follow practices that an individual can do on their own. In this way, more people can potentially have access to the benefits of adopting these habits and become self-empowered by doing so.

In the bigger picture, this book has been written to support the dissemination of these practices to a wider audience and thereby help to increase the amount of happiness and positive action in the world.

DO NOT SEARCH OR WAIT FOR HAPPINESS

"Happiness is an inside job." – William Arthur Ward

One thing I would really like to impress upon you is that it is important to understand that happiness is found in the here and now. Please do not get lost in the "search for happiness" which is an idea that infers that happiness will hopefully occur at some point in the future and that it comes from outside.

Happiness is found inside yourself. It is not solely due to outside factors. In fact, it has been calculated that our circumstances can only be accountable for a maximum of 10% of our happiness.

Our outside situation does not have to define our lives.

There is an inspiring book called "Man's Search for Meaning" written by Viktor Frankl which highlights this in the most extreme circumstances. Viktor was an Austrian professor of Psychology who was interned in Auschwitz during World War 2 because he was Jewish. Despite being in this awful situation he chose to use the experience as an opportunity to learn about and understand our human capacity to survive in such atrocious conditions. He elected to do this because he was already trained to study human behavior and also because he was fascinated to observe that some of the internees seemed to be able to choose to remain kind and open-hearted despite their dire situation whilst others succumbed to despair. The former had much higher survival rates. The difference was the way that they perceived their situation and purpose in life or value to others.

There is a deeply moving 1998 Italian movie called "Life is Beautiful" which is a tragicomic tale following the story of a man and his son who also end up in a concentration camp in World War 2. In the story, the father makes the whole experience less of a trauma for his son by looking for the humor and pretending that it is all a game. Although the movie weaves from being deeply sad to very funny and it seems quite unlikely, it is actually loosely based on the true story of Rubino Romeo Salmoni.

So the next time that you find yourself believing that you are unhappy because of your situation, try to remember that you too have a choice and can choose to find ways of being or thinking that can actually lead to a happier state of being – despite your circumstances.

From another perspective, happiness is not just something to be found inside yourself but is actually the nature of your true state of being. Therefore, the exercises in this book are not so much about helping you to be happier but actually about helping you to remember the natural state of happiness that is your birthright. They also train and empower you to be able to consciously reconnect with that happiness in the now and not to hope that happiness will happen to you at some point in the future.

WHAT IS HAPPINESS?

"The basic thing is that everyone wants happiness, no one wants suffering. And happiness mainly comes from our own attitude, rather than from external factors. If your own mental attitude is correct, even if you remain in a hostile atmosphere, you feel happy." – The Dalai Lama

This is an important question to look at before we proceed much further because happiness means different things to different people and in different contexts.

To a degree, it can be misleading because we sometimes attempt to appear happy as a way of avoiding the uncomfortable feelings that we are really experiencing. We might also pursue instant but fleeting pleasure or sometimes addictive state changing experiences to try to escape difficult emotions.

The approach that I am recommending has nothing to do with avoidance and has everything to do with being emotionally authentic and having the skills and habits that support us to move through challenging situations so that we are able to spend more of our time in positive states of being.

In fact, a really important part of the process of becoming happier is to recognize, embrace and appropriately express all of our emotional states. Inherently suffering, pain and negativity are naturally part of life. Knowing that this is the case and accepting it as such, can stop us from getting caught in the futile struggle of desperately trying to avoid the inevitable.

Part of this journey is about developing and cultivating habits that enable us to move through these negative states quickly and not to become stuck there. It is also about developing resilience skills and behaviors that enable us to deal with the inevitable knocks, pains, and challenges in life more effectively, so that we can quickly return to a more positive emotional way of being.

"Authentic happiness involves living a life full of appreciation, being mindful of each and every moment and passionately pursuing knowledge, friendships, health and career goals." – Martin Seligman

---

Martin Seligman defined 3 different types of happiness: pleasure, engagement, and meaning. He noted that each level becomes deeper and more profound.

The first type of happiness is attained by pursuing pleasure and it was shown to be the most fleeting and transient. This is the hedonistic pursuit of happiness that so frequently defines our modern Western society's way of being. It is often characterized by the belief that if we have, buy or own more, we will find happiness. Inevitably such feelings of raised happiness seldom last for long. In fact, when the impact of such pleasures were measured they were rarely found to last more than a few weeks at best and often just a few hours.

A classic example of the transient and impermanent nature of such happiness is the fact that people who win the lottery have been found to either return to the original level of life satisfaction that they had before winning or even to have increased levels of depression (and higher suicide rates) afterward. They are also likely to have lost their fortune within two years. This is because we all have "set points" for our levels of happiness and wealth and if we do not actively change the inner conditioning that created them, we will unconsciously return to them.

The second type is the engagement level of happiness (living the *"good life."*) It is experienced by being completely absorbed in an activity sometimes referred to as the "flow state." This is a state of timeless focus, connection and being authentically oneself. It was found to create higher levels of happiness that had a greater impact on people's lives and moods for longer periods of time.

The third type of happiness was engendered by altruistic behavior or living in a way that had real meaning and was for the greater good. This *"meaningful life"* seemed to create the longest lasting and most impactful levels of joy. The happiest and most successful people were seen to be the ones who lived life with engagement, meaning and contribution or a sense of service as a fundamental part of their daily experience.

"Positive states," "positivity" or "positive emotions" are in some way better terms to use than "happiness" because they do not lead to the idea that we are supposed to have a happy face at all times (even though we may well be much happier for more of the time through using these principles) and because they cover a broader range of the qualities of optimal living.

The researcher Barbara Fredrickson has defined the ten most common positive emotions as: "joy, gratitude, serenity, interest, hope, pride, amusement, inspiration, awe and love."

These are the array of emotions that we are seeking to expand. Firstly because they feel great and secondly because of the beneficial impact that being in these states will have on our lives.

THE FACEBOOK HAPPINESS TRAP AND OTHER STRESSES

A recent phenomenon that has greatly impacted young people is what I have termed the *Facebook Happiness Trap*. By this, I am referring to the pressure to always look like one is happy and having a great time on any photos and comments that are posted on Facebook or other social media sites. The very way that these platforms were designed has not encouraged the expression of the full spectrum of life's emotions and experiences. As a consequence, there is an increasing amount of stress and emotional challenge experienced by teenagers and young adults.

Various studies have shown that this rise in stress levels can be traced to the necessity to be seen to be constantly happy on social media and an increased tendency to compare ourselves to more people (due to TV and the Internet bringing many more people into our daily experience than our ancestors had to relate to).

There are also another couple of factors that have resulted in increasingly stressed children. In schools, there has been an greater than ever focus on constantly achieving higher grades, both for children and teachers. Such pressure is not conducive to success, creativity or happiness, and one has to wonder about the lack of government wisdom in the face of all of the modern research that shows that this approach is so detrimental to healthy and successful education.

The other growing contemporary stress is due to a trend of parents overprotecting their children which has resulted in them being less able to cope with the normal challenges of growing up. As a consequence, levels of depression and the need for counseling support for teenagers have risen quite dramatically.

In recognition of this, helping children to embrace all of the emotional aspects of life, to develop resilience skills and to access real happiness through their habits can be invaluable.

PERHAPS CONTENTMENT IS A BETTER WORD

In some ways, having the goal of developing our ability to be content is perhaps more useful than getting caught in thinking that you must always be happy, ecstatic and joyful. Although these emotions are all fabulous and they become more accessible as you go on this journey, it is your capacity to remain positive and OK with more situations as they arise that will be of greatest benefit for you. This sense of ease and resilience will enable you to navigate the inevitable misfortunes and adversities that come your way, as well as to be OK with what is. Understanding and practicing the happiness habits will inevitably enable you to live in a state of greater contentment.

The sage advice for the need to simply learn to be more content can be found in some of our ancient and esteemed philosophical and spiritual teachings.

> *"True happiness is to enjoy the present, without anxious dependence upon the future, not to amuse ourselves with either hopes or fears but to rest satisfied with what we have, which is sufficient, for he that is so wants nothing. The greatest blessings of mankind are within us and within our reach. A wise man is content with his lot, whatever it may be, without wishing for what he has not."* – Seneca

The Stoic school of thought that developed in ancient Greece and Rome was a deeply, well-considered tradition that believed that finding contentment by living the *good life* was the ultimate goal.

> *"Health is the greatest gift,*
> *Contentment is the greatest wealth."*
> – Gautama Buddha

The Buddha taught that we are unhappy in life because we are always looking for, craving and attempting to hold on to satisfaction from sources outside of ourselves, which by their very nature will always change and end. As such, our attachment to them will always result in some degree of misery. The key to overcoming this "suffering" and to find peace and contentment is to let go of all desire and clinging.

"Be content with what you have;
rejoice in the way things are.
When you realize there is nothing lacking, the
whole world belongs to you." – Lao Tzu

The ancient Chinese philosophy of Taoism also encourages us to find joy and contentment in life as it is and to trust in the way of nature.

WHY SHOULD WE CHOOSE TO BE HAPPIER?

There have been many studies and research projects over the last couple of decades that have looked at the impact of being happier on people's lives. In 2005 Lyubomirsky, King and Diener wrote a paper entitled *"The Benefits of Frequent Positive Affect: Does Happiness Lead to Success?"* which was a meta-analysis (a comparative evaluation of over 200 studies that assessed over 275,000 people). It concluded that **increased happiness led to increased success and fulfillment in nearly every aspect of life including work, career, health, marriage, relationships, friendships, community and creativity.**

These studies all showed that we gain an incredible amount of benefits above and beyond just the present moment experience of happiness.

One of the other aspects of the findings of these research projects is that the improved levels of success and fulfillment were caused by living in a happier or more positive way first and not the other way around!

This means that **happiness is an enabler**. The more that someone is able to maintain positive states, the greater their capacity to do well in pretty much all areas of their lives!

I'M SURE I WOULD BE HAPPIER IF I HAD MORE MONEY

"What's the use of happiness? It can't buy you money."
– Henry Youngman

When I was 20 I left the UK to travel and work my way around the world, as my last chance for adventure before I joined the pursuit of a career, family, and monetary acquisition. What started as a dream of staying away for a whole year ended up turning into ten amazing years of my life. Apart from discovering what an incredibly beautiful planet we live on and realizing that it is populated by 99.99% wonderful, generous, warm-hearted and fascinating individuals, I also learned a lot about our different ways of living in and perceiving this world.

One of the things that intrigued me was that some of the happiest people I met were often some of the poorest ones. I vividly remember the first time that this struck me.

I was in Egypt, it was sunrise and I was up early to go on a donkey trip (not a particularly comfortable mode of transport) to the Valley of the Kings. As I walked towards the morning rendezvous point I noticed some freshly awakened street vendors who had slept the night next to the road wrapped in carpets. They unrolled themselves from said carpets and laid out the few objects that they intended to sell that day. I was particularly struck by the sight of one man who had a row of about 20 Bic pens for sale and an incredibly wide and bright smile. He wasn't smiling because he wanted me to buy a pen. He was smiling at and with all the other street vendors who seemed to be delighted to have woken up in that dusty and exotic world. He just seemed to be happy to be alive, to have friends, a carpet, and 20 cheap plastic pens!

I had countless experiences like this where I would meet people who from a Western perspective would have been seen to be poor and unfortunate yet seemed incredibly happy and to be really enjoying their lives.

Bizarrely, there was also a tendency that I noticed when spending time with rich and affluent groups of people for them to seem much less happy and be very stressed about life.

I hasten to add that these are of course generalizations because there are also many unhappy poor people and happy rich people too. It was just that until my early travels I had believed that it was imperative to accumulate wealth if you wanted to be happy.

This made no sense to me at first but it certainly did fascinate me and inspired me to try to understand what enabled people to be happy.

Then, of course, there was my own experience. I spent most of those ten years living on a shoestring, working for limited periods of time and going on as many adventures as I could in between. I had very few possessions (because I would have had to carry them in my backpack) and did not accumulate large amounts of money, yet these were some of the happiest years of my life.

Numerous studies of wealth and happiness have found little correlation between them except for in the following three instances:

- if people in extreme poverty are enabled to get themselves out of that extreme and challenging state

- if we spend money on experiences and activities rather than things

- if we spend money on others especially if it is to help them in some way.

Conversely, it has been found that being unhappy can actually have a negative impact on your capacity to earn money. In a study by Jan Emmanuel De Neve, he found that unhappy students earned 30% less income than their fellow classmates ten years later in life!

"STATIC HAPPINESS"

Sociologists measuring general levels of happiness in modern Western societies have also discovered that we are presently in a state of "Static Happiness." Our happiness levels have not increased at all in the past 50 years despite the many technological advances, a five fold rise in average household income and the ever growing amount of consumables and services that we now have in our lives.

It turns out that community and social connection (which is often still very strong in poor communities), how we view and appreciate life and our learned capacity to cope with its challenges (our resilience), as well as our habits of physical exercise (once known as using your body in day to day natural living), sleeping properly and diet, have a far greater impact on our ability to be happy in life than how much money we have.

THE "SUCCESS AND OWNERSHIP LEAD TO HAPPINESS" FORMULA IS WRONG!

The common belief is that when we succeed, achieve or own certain things we will become happier and more positive. Our whole modern world's thinking is based on this premise which is why we are endlessly attempting to get, have and be more. Yet it turns out that this formula is back to front – the happier people are to begin with, the more likely they are to be successful, effective, creative and ultimately content in life.

The "happiness after goal achievement" model also rarely works for long because so often in today's world the goalposts and levels of achievement required are constantly changed in a relentless push for greater productivity. As a result, we never actually get to the elusive "there" that we believed was going to give us happiness.

There is also a similarity here with the "retirement mentality" – a putting off enjoyment now until we retire at 65 years old. This can be a tragedy for two reasons. Firstly, 36% of people will have died before they get to 65 years old and will never have the chance to even try being totally free to enjoy themselves. Secondly, having spent 45 or so years of their lives not choosing to enjoy themselves it can be difficult to retrain oneself to get back into or learn how to make more fulfilling choices in life, i.e. "you can't teach an old dog new tricks." (Although that this is not completely accurate due to our brain's plasticity which enables us to constantly learn. However, it does require conscious retraining and the earlier you start the better.)

The similarity with overcoming the retirement mentality is that the more that we consciously practice choosing happier and more positive states of mind, the easier it becomes to drop into those states and to maintain them.

In reality, we are much more likely to succeed and achieve if we have actively chosen to live in a more positive way to start with.

OUR "HAPPINESS SET POINT"

It appears that we actually all have set points for the level of happiness that we are used to having and therefore that we are comfortable with. This is in effect the general level of happiness that we have maintained throughout our lives and is mostly reflective of our conditioning – the beliefs, habits, thoughts, emotional patterns and attitudes that we learned, heard, experienced, witnessed and modeled whilst we grew up.

These set points are like a thermostat that always returns us to the same level to which it has been programmed. If it gets too hot a thermostat will turn the heating off. If it gets too cold the thermostat will turn the heating up. Similarly, your inner set point will keep you roughly at the same level of happiness that you are used to maintaining – unless you adjust it.

The good news is that we can adjust our inner happiness thermostats! They have been set at their present level by our habitual ways of perceiving, thinking and doing things. Therefore, when we change some of these thoughts, perceptions and activities, our set points will subsequently be modified too. In essence, this is what many of the exercises in this book will be doing for you.

So Why Aren't We Happier?

Before I explore the various ways to increase happiness and positivity in your life, I am going to investigate some of the main reasons why so many of us are not happy. Understanding what these reasons are may help you to question some really important unexamined assumptions about life and to start raising your capacity to choose to be happier.

The pursuit of happiness or the wish to be happier would seem to be a universal desire that all humans around the planet are driven by on an innate level. Yet if it is a collective urge that we all have why does it not appear to be humanity's dominant emotion? Beyond that question, we must also look at whether it should indeed be our foremost emotion?

This is an important question because I want to restate that I am not suggesting that you should be happy, happy, happy all of the time or that you should pretend that you are happy by putting a happy face on whatever you are really feeling or that you should succumb to the Facebook happiness trap dilemma.

It is incredibly important for us to give ourselves permission to feel the emotions that we label as being negative because if we do not allow ourselves to feel these emotions then we will be less able to feel our positive emotions too. If we suppress some emotions we suppress our capacity to feel *all* of our emotions!

We are subject to an array of emotions that make up the experience of being human and it is really important that we allow ourselves to feel those emotions and are authentic in our appropriate expression of them.

However, we can get unnecessarily stuck in negative ways of thinking and feeling which will massively impair our ability to be successful, effective, creative, healthy and of course... happy.

I am going to look into some of the main reasons that we struggle to find happiness because through understanding these reasons they are likely to lose some of their power over us.

OUR FEAR WIRING

There are two main parts of our brains that are set up for the fear response due to the necessity of being able to recognize and deal with dangerous and life-threatening situations in our human development. The first part is the amygdala which is designed to recognize situations and patterns in our environment that are potentially dangerous. The second is the brain stem, which is the oldest part of our brains and is sometimes known as our lizard brain. It triggers our instant fight, flight or freeze reactions to situations that are perceived as threatening.

Both of these parts of the brain are associated with the emotion of fear. Without these responses, our ancestors would not have been able to survive in what was often a challenging and dangerous world. These reactions were so important that our brains are wired to actually pay more attention to things which are negative or potentially threatening and also to remember them for longer.

Have you ever wondered why despite having childhoods that consisted mostly of good experiences, people more easily remember the very scary or bad moments vividly but fewer of the good ones? It is because evolutionarily, our ancestors needed to clearly remember any experiences that were dangerous so that they had a better chance of responding appropriately to any similar situations in the future. In this way, our chances of survival were increased.

It is also worth noting that the stress hormones that are released as a result of these ancient reactions are often not appropriate or helpful in the face of the kinds of stresses that affect us in the modern world like deadlines, debt, etc. They often end up causing ill health because these stressors are constant and ongoing. The stress hormones instruct your body to send blood to its extremities (your limbs – so that you are better able to fight or flee) and away from your brain which means that you are less able to think clearly – it has been shown that people's IQs actually drop when in a stress response state.

These parts of the brain are also unable to see or allow for conse-quences and can keep you locked into cycles of desire and addiction via the release of dopamine. Habits like getting unconsciously lost on Facebook for hours, excessive bad food cravings and shopping addic-tions are great examples of dopamine-inspired actions where we do not seem to have any control over our actions in the moment.

The good news is that there is another part of our brain where our intelligence and reason reside. It is called the prefrontal cortex or neocortex. This is our higher brain center and it has the capacity to override these fear responses as well as give us clarity and the ability to overrule such cravings.

It is mostly through the practice of shifting our conscious thinking to the neocortex that enables us to rest in more positive emotional states. This is our practice and our goal.

THE NEGATIVE TO POSITIVE RATIO

As I just mentioned we are wired to respond more quickly to the nega-tive things in our environments than the positive. However, there is a tipping point in the ratio of good to bad things at which we are natu-rally drawn into being more positive, optimistic and happy. That ratio is 3:1 or 3 positive comments, experiences or interactions to every 1 negative experience. This is known as the Losada line (it was discov-ered by Marcial Losada).

In fact for optimal positivity and effectiveness a ratio of 6:1 was found to be best.

But please note that these ratios do not preclude having negativity in your life. There will always be negative and challenging situations. The goal is to minimize them, to learn to become more resilient, effective and creative at dealing with them and also to bring in more positives to your reality so that you are better able to deal with anything.

THE FEAR BASED MEDIA INDUSTRY

One of our challenges is that our media is obsessed with promoting fear and negativity which can have a massive adverse impact on our thoughts, feelings and our environments too. News channels are generally biased to the political system and country within which they exist and which they support.

As I mentioned in the introduction, I had the privilege to travel around the world for many years and was often fascinated by how differently various country's media would describe the same events (and my experience was that even in what we think of as the Western, free, democratic countries, the news was definitely biased and distorted too). I must also add that I particularly enjoyed living in countries where I could not speak the language well enough to understand the negativity and constant marketing propaganda that was bombarding everyone else.

It is poignant to note that studies have found that people who do not watch TV are more able to accurately assess the nature of various situations whereas people who watch TV regularly are more likely to have a negatively skewed view of reality.

You might wonder why our media promotes so much negativity. The short answer is because it sells! Negative news headlines catch our attention more. As the old media adage goes *"bad news is good news!"*

Similarly, advertising is often very effective because it makes us feel that we are not good enough or that we do not have enough (which are fear thought patterns). It then leads us to believe that if we were to just buy the products being promoted we could fix those inadequacies. Invariably it does not fulfill its promises.

Many TV shows and films stimulate fear, tension and our adrenal responses. I sometimes wonder if this is attractive to many of us because in normal life we can end up living in quite numb and disconnected ways. Such forms of entertainment can break through the numbness and allow us to feel more intense moments, even if only briefly.

However, as stated, the challenge with all of this outside negative information is that it does have a massive impact on us and our ability to be positive and happy. To rebalance the situation we need to consciously choose to have more positive experiences and thought patterns whilst at the same time finding ways to reduce the negative external information that we receive.

Some of the most productive and happy people I know have actually not got televisions and refuse to read newspapers. That may seem like a radical option to you at present but it does not mean that you have to have your head in the sand – it is still possible to discover what is happening and relevant to you with the Internet and in conversations with discerning friends.

POOR DIET AND HEALTH

Our state of health can also have a huge impact on how we feel and think. We all know that an achy, long-lasting flu experience can be debilitating on an emotional and mental level as much as on the physical level. But many people do not see or recognize the impact of the long-term, insidious effects of eating the average Western diet and not doing some form of regular exercise.

The modern Western diet (amusingly called the "Standard American Diet" or SAD in the USA) is excessively high in carbohydrates, sugars, and meat products whilst being low in nutrients, good fats, fruits and vegetables. This kind of diet is cheap to make, mass produce and make profits from, especially because it induces repetitive buying. Sugar and simple carbs are both highly addictive, in fact, sugar has been found to be 8 times more addictive than cocaine when tested on mice!

The SAD diet is very lucrative for the food manufacturers but has resulted in a massive increase in the amount of sugar consumed by the average person and has had a shocking impact on the general population's health, as can be seen by the rising levels of diabetes, obesity, cancer, heart disease, etc.

LACK OF EXERCISE

Our bodies have also evolved over tens of thousands of years in environments where we used them for carrying, lifting, digging, hunting, running, etc. They function much more efficiently on many levels when they are being physically active, yet in today's modern world many of us hardly exercise or use our bodies properly at all.

Exercise also stimulates the release of hormones and chemicals that cause feelings of happiness whilst at the same time breaking down stress hormones.

Because many people have a poor diet and a lack of exercise their health is far below its optimal level and this certainly has an impact on their ability to be and stay positive.

DISCONNECTION

Another challenge that we have in our modern world is that many of us are not living naturally in regards to our social connections. Humans have lived for hundreds of years within deeply interconnected small communities where mutual support, understanding, and knowing our purpose and place within those communities, were normal and integral to the way that we lived.

There was a fascinating study entitled *"Very Happy People"* done in 2002 by M. Seligman and E. Diener. They wanted to uncover what were the things that the top 10% of the happiest Americans had in common. They looked at various factors such as their level of wealth, health, the climate that they lived in, etc. Incredibly, they discovered that only one commonality stood out for them all – the fact that they had strong social relationships! This one aspect of their lives was far more influential than anything else.

Today, despite being able to connect with millions of people at the touch of a button via the Internet and telecommunications technology, we presently have the highest levels of loneliness and depression since we first began to record these measurements. These are conditions that are often remedied by having close and supportive social connections. So despite us now being able to have large social cyber networks, they do not seem to be able to fulfill the same valuable role as having real people that we closely relate to in our daily lives.

A supportive community of friends, colleagues and family can help us with our challenges, offer us various viewpoints, encourage us, celebrate our achievements and share experiences of fun and joy with us. The positive impact of these interactions is well worth actively pursuing.

Many people are quite disconnected from themselves due to living in a modern society that focuses on the power of the mind and logic (at the expense of the heart and emotional intelligence) and of the external, the man-made and "superficial" world. Also, many of us live in towns and cities where most of the natural world has been removed or covered with concrete and therefore we can be very disconnected from nature. Throughout our human history, we have spent most of our time in the natural world, so it seems inevitable that separating ourselves from that reality was bound to create some problems.

We forget that we are a part of nature and instead get caught in the illusion that we are above it and actually its masters. This naïve and somewhat arrogant perspective has led us to a place and time when we could actually be the cause of mass planetary extinction unless we quickly become consciously aware and actively choose to make big changes to the way that we are living.

Reconnecting with the natural world is an invaluable way to gain a clearer perspective. There is something incredibly healing and balancing about the experience of consciously spending time in nature. Whether it is for playing sports, going hiking, gardening or watching a stunning sunset, these experiences support us to feel our sense of connection with the world around us and to be happier.

ADDICTIVE PATTERNS

Bizarrely we are often addicted to unhappy patterns or to habits that stop us from fully feeling our emotions – a strategy that actually ends up dulling all of the emotions.

One addiction that is rarely noticed is the addiction to drama. This has also been found to be more addictive than cocaine! It is addictive because of the sensations caused by the adrenaline that is released which lead to a sense of significance and connection (with other people addicted to drama). However, drama gets directly in the way of happiness and fulfillment.

Other addictions such as food, alcohol, cigarettes, TV, sex, FB or whatever we find ourselves unconsciously doing, inhibit our ability to feel and are inherently disempowering.

To clarify what I mean when I refer to an addiction I am referring to any habit that we use to help us change our emotional state because we do not like the feelings and thoughts that we are experiencing. Such a strategy is unfortunately only slightly helpful in the short term and is destructive and very unhelpful in the long term. If we reduce our ability to feel difficult emotions we also lessen our capacity to feel positive emotions.

The only viable way to actually overcome addictions from this perspective is to learn to go through or express these emotions in a safe and healthy way. This may involve getting professional help to clear past traumas, conditioning, fears, limiting patterns, etc. In some cases, it can be enough to just sit and be fully present with the uncomfortable feelings because when given space they will often dissipate or transform. Using either of these approaches can then allow us to experience our joy and other positive emotions more fully too.

HOW TO ACTUALLY BECOME HAPPIER – THE PRACTICES

> *"Happiness is a thing to be practiced, like the violin."*
> – John Lubbock

The following chapters are dedicated to various practices that have been proven to be very effective and valuable in enabling you to experience more positive emotions and happiness in an ongoing way. These exercises actually do not need to take very long to do at all and yet they can have an enormous impact on your mind, emotions, and well-being.

To get the most from this book, adopt at least a couple of practices to do on a daily basis for a few weeks, then see how you feel and what has changed for you. At that point, you are likely to find that you are enjoying the experience of your life much more and that these simple practices have become easy to sustain new habits. You can then build on top of these by trying other practices from this book and adding them into your life too. These will increase your joy, success, and appreciation even further.

You may find it helpful to know that **being happier is a process and an experience**. As you do these exercises regularly you will find that your happiness set point will shift so that you experience more positive emotional states more often. At the same time as your overall capacity to be happy increases, you will also become aware that these exercises enable you to be happier more often and for longer periods.

It is important to realize that **it is often the small changes that you make and practice regularly that have the biggest impact.**

In Chapter 11, Jumpstart Your Joy, you will learn a couple of simple habits you can easily do every day that can have a profound impact on your life. This chapter is really designed to inspire and enable you to take action and make changes right now. These practices are especially potent because they are designed to make it effortless for you to integrate simple positive habits into your life and then quickly experience how they affect your emotional and mental states and raise your happiness levels. This is both empowering and inspiring because you will realize that you can control your state and, therefore, choose to live more happily.

Remember that as a result of feeling and being more positive and happy on an ongoing basis you are much more likely to experience increased success and fulfillment in nearly every aspect of life including work, career, health, marriage, relationships, friendships, community and creativity. The following chapters provide you with the simple tools to make this your reality...

PART 2

THE PRACTICES

CHAPTER 2. GRATITUDE AND APPRECIATION

– The Foundation Stones Of Happiness

"Gratitude is not only the greatest of virtues but the parent of all the others." – Marcus Tullius Cicero (106-43 BC)

These are definitely the most important practices to integrate on a daily basis. Although gratitude and appreciation are similar in nature I am going to define them as slightly different from each other in the context of these exercises.

Gratitude is a feeling of thankfulness for things, people, situations, and experiences in our lives.

Appreciation, on the other hand, infers being grateful for something or someone and evaluating how and why it is of such value. It may also be less personal i.e. it can encompass things, actions, and people out in the world that do not directly impact us yet nevertheless we value and are grateful for – the work that they do, who they are, what they are, etc.

An inherently important part of the process of appreciation can be an expression of thanks to anyone who is associated with making those things or experiences that we are appreciative of, come to pass. I call it *active appreciation* when we take time to directly express appreciation to others and I highly recommend doing so because of the positive ripple effect that it causes in our circles of influence.

THE IMPACT OF GRATITUDE AND APPRECIATION

As mentioned in the first chapter we have several challenges that generally keep us focused on the negative side of our reality. Primarily these are: that our brains are wired to look for negative and dangerous situations and secondly that our modern society is caught in the "more is better" paradigm which can leave us constantly in a state of lack and "not enough." However, regularly practicing gratitude and appreciation can totally reverse this negative bias because we begin to bring our focus on all that we *have* in our lives, not on what we *don't have*.

Generally the more that we practice this the more we discover that we have an immense amount of things to be grateful for already. Once we start finding and appreciating these positive things and experiences we then start to tip the balance of positives to negatives in our lives too. (Remember the Losada line?) We need to have at least 3 positive experiences to every negative one to be our most productive, successful and happy.

One of the keys that support this process is that we do the gratitude exercise first thing in the morning.

Life Key: whatever we do first thing in the morning after we wake up, primes our subconscious mind to work in a similar way throughout the day.

Therefore, if you spend 5 minutes to search your memories for things that you can be grateful for, you will discover that you have a tendency to unconsciously do this throughout the day. Plus you might find that you are consciously looking out for positive experiences and moments that you can appreciate to write down later.

In effect, you are using brain plasticity to your advantage as you re-program and retrain your mind to search, find and acknowledge the good things in life.

There is also a ripple effect that results from us expressing our appreciation directly to others. When we do this, not only do we feel good but the recipients feel seen, valued and appreciated, which in turn will boost their happiness and well-being too! In this way, gratitude fosters and increases social connections, friendship, trust, and co-operation. Indeed, it is a social emotion that has been imperative for the formation and maintenance of communities throughout our human history.

GRATITUDE RESEARCH

There have been numerous studies that have looked at the impact of simple daily gratitude and appreciation practices which have shown how effective and powerful they are. Many research projects have looked at the very practical use of gratitude exercises to greatly reduce or clear depression in chronically depressed people. In fact, this was often found to be more effective than the potentially harmful anti-depressants that are regularly given to people suffering from depression.

In 2005, an empirical validation of the effectiveness of various positive psychology interventions was carried out (*American Psychologist July-Aug 2005 by Seligman, Steen, Park and Peterson*). The most effective practice was an exercise called "Three Good Things in Life" where the participants were asked to write down three things that went well each day and their causes every night for one week. Not only did these people have increased levels of happiness and less depression at the time but these levels remained high even 6 months later!

"I don't have to chase extraordinary moments to find happiness – it's right in front of me if I'm paying attention and practicing gratitude." – Brene Brown.

In 2015, an interesting study of the actual neurological process of being grateful by means of MRI was completed. This marks a shift from the more plentiful social science-based studies of gratitude to a more medical and anatomical science-based research. The *Neural Correlates of Gratitude* study was carried out by R. Glen Fox et al to ascertain if the experience of gratitude could be measured in the brain. Indeed it was possible. They found that the regions associated with moral cognition and value judgment in the brain would light up in response to the feelings of gratitude.

It is a pity that they did not scan the heart at the same time, as this has a very concentrated surrounding neural network which does a lot of the information processing once assumed to be the sole domain of the brain. As it is generally our heart region that we tend to feel emotions of joy and happiness in and around, it would seem to me that measuring changes in this area would have been far more interesting.

MORNING GRATITUDE JOURNALING

This exercise is best done when you first wake up. Have a pen and a journal that is just for writing your gratitudes and appreciations in, next to your bed. If you use an alarm and have limited time in the morning then you may need to set it 5-10 minutes earlier so that you can do this exercise in a stress-free way.

Write down at least 3 things that you can be grateful for in your life. These things do not have to be really big things (although they can be of course), they may be as simple as a smile from a stranger, a moment of sunshine, a good friend, a completed job, the clean bedsheets that you slept in, the roof over your head, last night's dinner, your job, passing an exam, etc. They may have happened very recently or a long time ago.

Whatever pops into your mind is good. Write it down and take a moment to ponder why you are grateful for it and how that recognition makes you feel inside physically.

Be committed to yourself to write at least 3 different things that you are grateful for every day. It can be valuable for at least one of these things to be for some very simple everyday experience whilst the other gratitudes can be for bigger things. Over time, you may find that you have more things that you recognize that you are grateful for and that you want to write down each day, so do feel free to do so if you have time.

It can be helpful to begin the process directly when you awaken and are still lying in bed. Start to search your mind and memories for things that you can be grateful for in your life to write in your journal as soon as you get up.

Certainly keeping a gratitude journal in this way is probably the most effective technique to consciously develop a grateful mindset but it is also possible to use environmental triggers to remind you of the good things in your life. An environmental trigger is something that occurs quite regularly in life, such as when you hear the new text tone on your phone or whenever you find yourself waiting in a queue. These moments might just pass you by or even be a source of annoyance normally. However, if you decide that they are now an opportunity to acknowledge new things that you are grateful for elsewhere in your life, these moments can be totally transformed.

THE EVENING "MAGIC MOMENTS" EXERCISE

Every night just before going to sleep or whenever is convenient for you in the evening, use a journal to write down 1-3 magical moments from your day. These good or special experiences can range from having been simple and brief to maybe even incredible and awesome, just as long as they inspire an inner heart smile when you think back to them. After each good thing that you write down, take a moment to ponder whether anyone else was involved who enabled the experience or thing to happen. Also, consider which of your own qualities facilitated it happening. Make a brief note of that too. (Whenever you can in the following days, tell any relevant people that you appreciate them for who they are or what they did.)

That's it. It is as simple as that! In a similar way to how the morning gratitude exercise works on your subconscious mind throughout the day, this evening exercise can have a very positive impact on your dreaming mind and the quality of your sleep. It will make the process of being grateful in the morning easier too.

PRACTICING APPRECIATION WITH OTHERS

There is another way to do this exercise but with other people such as your children or your partner so that it has a great effect on them as well.

SHARED APPRECIATION

Simply take time in the evening or just before sleep to share favorite magical moments of the day. Take turns and share 1, 2 or 3 of these experiences with each other, saying what they were, why you appreciated them and perhaps who was involved that helped these things happen. Such a practice can have a profound effect on your relationships. Children often really love to do this.

It must be noted that if you have children, inspiring them to think in this way on a daily basis could be one of the best things that you could teach them for the rest of their lives.

SAVORING THE MOMENT

"The best way to pay for a lovely moment is to enjoy it."
– Richard Bach

This is an optional practice that I wanted to mention here, as although it is an incredibly valuable and effective thing to do, I would rather that you just noticed it happening and enjoyed the experience instead of seeing it as an exercise that you need to schedule into your day and commit to.

Savoring a moment is all about becoming very conscious and aware of a good experience as it is actually happening so that you can fully appreciate it in the moment. Often we miss these moments because our minds are in the habit of remembering past events or planning for future ones rather than being fully in the present or perhaps because we are so busy talking to other people at the same time that we miss it.

Again, these moments can be very simple such as experiencing a brief bit of sunshine on a rainy day, a break from work, the completion of a chore, a funny moment with friends, a beautiful experience in nature, etc.

You may consciously choose to savor such experiences in your day beforehand or you may just find yourself unconsciously becoming aware of such moments as a result of your mind learning to look for things that it can be grateful for or appreciate in your life to write in your journal later. Either way, your life will become more rich and enjoyable because of it.

> *"Plenty of people miss their share of happiness,*
> *not because they never found it, but because*
> *they didn't stop to enjoy it."* – William Feather

Here is a question that I recommend that you ask yourself before you leave home in the mornings:

"I wonder what I will savor and enjoy today?"

You may be surprised how easily such a simple question can enable your mind to seek and find amazing experiences. Try it for a week and see what happens.

GRATITUDE STONES AND OTHER TRIGGERS

Sometimes it can be useful to have triggers in our environments that remind us to stop and be grateful or to savor the moment. I know of people who keep a special stone in their pocket which prompts them to appreciate something whenever they touch it. For my own amusement, I sometimes keep a small toy Minion, who I have named Albert, in my pocket because every time that I notice him I can't help but smile.

Alternatively, you may use regularly recurring situations or sounds to remind you in a similar way. Occurrences that could potentially be annoying are particularly useful to do this with because they can be transformed into positive experiences e.g. TV adverts, a frozen or slow computer program, red traffic lights, text tones, etc. Find something that could work for you and try it out for a couple of days.

THE FOUNDATIONS OF A HAPPIER LIFE

Gratitude and appreciation are probably the most important things that you can do to change and improve your life. Ideally, it would be good to complete both the gratitude and the appreciation exercises each day, but if you do not think that you will do both to start with, then choose the one that appeals to you most and commit to doing it for a few weeks. You may find that its effect on your life inspires you to want to do both. Also using the *My Happiness Journal* can be really helpful for getting you started with these practices as the spaces for writing both practices are already prepared for you. You just have to fill them in.

REMEMBERING THE BIG PICTURE

Perhaps the most fundamental thing to be grateful for is life – your life and life on this planet. Somehow we can so easily take this for granted and not recognize how lucky we truly are. Planet Earth itself is stunningly beautiful in so many ways. It has an incredibly complex biosphere and fragile atmosphere that has wondrously enabled life to exist and thrive here.

The chances that we should end up alive on the only planet that we have discovered thus far capable of sustaining life is beyond miraculous. In fact, the odds against it happening makes winning the lottery, by comparison, look as easy as flipping a coin! Or perhaps considerably easier...

Just looking at one aspect of this miracle, the probability of you being born as the culmination of your ancestral lineage is quite staggering. Dr. Ali Binazir actually took the time to work out the fascinating odds of you being born as you from a purely statistical perspective. This is what he found...

A conservative estimate of the chance of your parents meeting each other is 1 in 20000. The chance of them staying together and having kids is about 1 in 2000. So far, that is a chance of 1 in 40 million. The odds against one specific egg and sperm coming together to make you out of the trillions of other ones that came from your parents is 1 in 400,000,000,000,000,000. The odds against your ancestor lineage remaining unbroken for the whole of human existence (approximately 150,000 generations) is about 1 in 10 with 45,000 zeroes after it. But the odds of the right sperm meeting the right egg each of those times is 1 in 10 with 2,640,000 zeroes after it. If you have lost track of these mind-boggling figures, that means the likelihood of you being born as you is equivalent to 1 in 10 with 2,685,000 zeroes after it. To put that into context, the number of atoms in the Earth is only 10 with 50 zeros after it. In other words, the chances of you being here now, as you are, is pretty much ZERO! You are indeed a living miracle!

Even without diving into your deepest ancestral history, you are likely to be incredibly fortunate. We assess how well we are doing by comparing ourselves to the people directly around us (which unfortunately can now include the ones that we see on television too), so we do not normally get a sense of the bigger picture. Our human family presently consists of about 7 billion people, the majority of whom are very far away from your immediate reality. However, I am going to share some facts that will perhaps give you a sense of where you might be in relationship to them in the big picture.

- The global median income is $1,225 per year.

- Half of the world's richest people in the top 1% live in the USA (and you only need to earn over $34,000 to be in that top 1%!)

- Half of the world's population are unemployed.

- 1 in 3 people do not have access to adequate sanitation.

- only 6.7% of the world's population has a college degree.

- 16% of the world's population has no access to electricity.

If you have never really looked far beyond your neighborhood and your television screen to get a sense of your standing in the world, then these figures might just shift your perspective. You <u>are</u> incredibly lucky and there really is so much to be grateful for.

***

If you would like a great journal to write up you gratitudes and your magic moments the "My Happiness Journal" has been designed for this use. When you claim your happiness toolkit, you will be sent a coupon code to get the journal at a reduced price. To get your happiness toolkit go to the Reader Bonus Materials.

CHAPTER 3. MEDITATION

"True happiness is to enjoy the present, without anxious dependence upon the future." – Lucius Annaeus Seneca

In literally thousands of studies, the practice of meditation has been found to have a substantial impact on the emotional, physical and mental health of people who practice it regularly. In some fascinating research that involved doing brain scans of long-term meditators and Buddhist monks, it was discovered that their left prefrontal cortexes (the part of our brains that are most associated with the emotion of happiness and compassion) were much larger and more developed due to their regular meditation practice!

Practicing meditation regularly, even if for relatively short periods, can have a profound effect on your well-being and happiness.

BUT WHAT IS MEDITATION?

Meditation has been used for thousands of years within different traditions around the world. In its essence, it is a spiritual practice to enable you to become more deeply connected to yourself and the world around you. Because there are numerous traditions within which meditative practices have arisen and millions of people who have developed these practices, there are literally thousands of forms of meditation.

This is rather useful because it means that in this modern world of easy information access and sharing, you can explore many meditative techniques to find ones that work for you.

The many varieties of meditation practice include watching the breath, repeating words in your mind (a mantra), staring at objects, slow conscious movement, making sounds, listening to sounds, sitting, standing, walking, etc. Despite the many differences, all of these many varied forms have one commonality – they are all about becoming fully aware in the present moment.

In some ways, it is actually useful to understand meditation as a way to train the mind so that it is able to rest in this present moment, to quieten down and be less active.

We often get caught in the unexamined belief that we *are* our minds and the things that we think. In actual fact, our mind is just a tool that enables us to process information in a certain way. When we learn to meditate we start to realize that we are more than just our minds and as we get in touch with this larger perspective we naturally connect with feelings of great inner peace and contentedness.

DO YOU HAVE TO BE RELIGIOUS OR SPIRITUAL TO MEDITATE?

Even though meditation has been traditionally mostly used as a spiritual practice it does not have to be used within that context at all. (Of course, if you do have a particular religious or spiritual belief then meditation can be very helpful to you.) Whether you have religious beliefs or not there are very beneficial effects that people receive from meditation.

WHAT ARE THE BENEFITS OF MEDITATION?

Research has shown that regular meditation has the following effects:

- ✓ increased happiness
- ✓ reduced stress
- ✓ boosted creativity
- ✓ improved memory and cognition
- ✓ improved concentration and focus
- ✓ boosted immunity
- ✓ better health and increased longevity

Those are seven fantastic reasons to explore and practice meditation in your daily life.

IS IT DIFFICULT TO MEDITATE?

I need to acknowledge that in the beginning meditation is not necessarily easy and often eludes people when they first attempt it. This is mostly because they have not learned proper ways to do it or because they have misleading expectations about what the meditative experience is supposed to be.

Most of us have untrained minds that have learned to do whatever they want, whenever they want and however they want. Consequently, it can take a while to learn how to still this unruly "thought factory"! However, the good news is that there are some very simple techniques that you can practice and some modern digitally supported ways to accelerate the learning process as well!

DOES MEDITATION TAKE A LOT OF TIME?

More good news is that it is not necessary to meditate for several hours each day just to learn how to do it and receive the benefits. Even 12-15 minutes per day will have a positive impact, especially if you do it first thing when you wake up. As I said in the last chapter – whatever you do first thing in the morning will create a pattern that your subconscious will repeat throughout the day.

I discovered how powerful and effective this was many years ago when I was experimenting with various types of meditations in the morning. One of the meditations that I would occasionally begin my day with was a laughing meditation which simply involved sitting up and laughing for the first 5 minutes of my day. Now you may think that it might be hard to laugh for no reason but actually, it sounds so ridiculous that it is quite funny which inspires real laughter. What was fascinating for me was that on the days that I did the laughter meditation, I noticed that I would laugh often throughout the day. When I became aware of this I then paid close attention to how whatever meditation, act or way of thinking I experienced upon first awakening would impact the rest of my day.

"Laughing is the best medicine – but if you are laughing for no reason you may need medicine." – Anon.

It turns out that the common English expression that warns about *getting out of bed on the wrong side* is accurate. If we wake up and begin focusing on the things that are creating stress in our lives then those negative, stressful thoughts will keep returning to us throughout the day. You may not have considered it before but if you find yourself hitting the alarm's snooze button you are unconsciously saying "I don't want to be awake/here/alive" and there is likely to be a theme of resistance to many of your experiences throughout the day.

So knowing that our first acts and thoughts have such a powerful influence on our days, it is worth consciously choosing a positive thing to do or think. This will enable our subconscious minds to support us by regularly returning us to that helpful way of being. Practicing meditation and gratitude upon waking are excellent ways to prepare yourself for more balanced, optimistic and happier days.

THREE SIMPLE MEDITATIONS

If you have not tried meditation before here are three simple meditations that you can try. Start with just meditating for 10 minutes and increase this amount of time as you are ready and able. Having a watch with a timer (there are some great meditation timer apps too) can be useful. It is best to practice meditating in a quiet environment that is free from distractions.

THE BREATH MEDITATION

Bring your awareness to your breath. Focus on a precise area of your breath such as your nostrils or the movement of your abdomen. Avoid changing your breathing – just become the observer of your breath as it is in the moment.

Be inquisitive as you discover more fully the nature of your breath. Listen to your breath. Feel your breath. Imagine the movement of your breath in your mind's eye. Pay attention to whether it is deep or shallow, fast or slow. Notice any pauses between your breaths. Be aware if your breathing changes at all.

Undoubtedly, your mind will wander and get distracted – this is the nature of the untrained mind. Your job is to realize when it has done so. Any time that you notice that your mind is distracted, just gently turn your attention back in that moment and refocus on your breath. Every time that you do so will strengthen your ability to keep returning to and being in the present.

The breath meditation is very valuable because it can be done anywhere and at any time, as a way of coming back to your center.

THE INNER SMILE MEDITATION

Sit in a comfortable position with your eyes closed. Bring your awareness to your face and gently smile. Notice the energy of your smile which you can experience as warmth and other sensations in your face. Now as you inhale draw that energy down into your heart and chest area. Be aware of the sensations in this area too. For 10 minutes, maintain a gentle smile on your lips and keep your awareness with the sensations that this generates across your face and in your chest.

I have created a very profound "Heart Meditation" which is available as a CD, that uses the inner smile as its foundation but then goes much deeper to enable healing, heart-opening, and an increased capacity to live in a more compassionate way. In the context of increasing your happiness, this form of *meta meditation* is very powerful because it will help you to develop your ability to be compassionate and as a re-

sult increase your willingness and enthusiasm to be kind to others. You will learn later that being kind in the world is a very powerful way to increase your own happiness and also the happiness of many people around you.

If you would like a copy to support you on your journey then go to

http://www.choosing-happier.com/heart-med

I am guessing that when you read my laughing meditation story you were probably intrigued to know what it might be like, so I encourage you to give it a go at least once. It can be a great way to bring more fun and humor into your life. The only thing that I would recommend is that if you sleep next to someone, you should explain to them in advance that you will be doing this meditation so that they do not wake up to the shock that you have cracked in the night! If you are lucky, they might be inspired to do the meditation with you which will make the experience even easier and more fun.

LAUGHTER MEDITATION

Set your intention the night before you go to sleep to wake up and laugh. This only has to be done for 5 minutes so it can be helpful to have a preset timer or a clock. Upon waking, sit up and try to laugh. You may find that remembering a funny incident can help this process or you may just want to bring your attention to the inner experience of laughter. Allow your laughter to generate more laughter. Notice the funny sounds that you make and the effect that the laughter is having on your body. After 5 minutes, stop laughing and just sit in silence for 1-2 minutes and be very conscious of the sensations within your body.

MODERN EASIER MEDITATION

If you want to learn how to meditate, it is best to do it in a class or on a retreat, where you can get direct guidance and feedback. However, it is also possible to practice on your own using techniques that you have learned or by using modern technology.

There are some very helpful meditation CDs available that you can use to support your practice. These may consist of relaxing music or spoken meditations. Guided meditations can be an easier way to start practicing meditating and focusing your mind (but listen to the person who is speaking on the recording first, to make sure that you like their voice for if you don't like it you will find it incredibly distracting).

Beyond CDs and digital meditation music, you may find that some of the meditation apps that are now available may be useful ways for you to practice and learn how to meditate. My favorite app is Headspace because it teaches the fundamentals of meditation in a very clear and accessible way.

It is also possible to use modern technology that has been developed to help you to automatically drop into a meditative state. One of my favorite technologies is a set of audio recordings with isochronic tones embedded into them which automatically lead you into a meditative state for 12 minutes at a time. You can find out more at http://modernmeditator.com/zen12. This is a great way to start the day but it can also be a fantastic way to take a break at any point during the day when you are struggling, tired or needing more focus.

If you would like to learn more about how to meditate and to get access to some great resources for making that process easier, go to the website www.modernmeditator.com. Have a browse through it, try some of the meditations and check out the Easy Meditation options so that you can start experiencing the benefits of meditation straight away.

***

There are several recorded MP3 meditation that you are able to download as part of the happiness toolkit for free. You might find these very useful to help you to meditate, especially if you are new to meditation To get your kit go to the Reader Bonus Materials.

CHAPTER 4. ACKNOWLEDGING YOUR STRENGTHS OF CHARACTER

"Be more concerned with your character than with your reputation. Your character is who you really are while your reputation is merely what others think of you." – John Wooden

It has been found that when we become clear about our natural character strengths and actively use them we boost our happiness, positivity, and effectiveness in life.

In the 2005 study of the efficacy of various positive psychology interventions that I mentioned in the Gratitude chapter, the second most effective positive psychology exercise was called "Using signature strengths in a new way." It involved a group discovering what their innate character strengths were and then finding new ways to use one of those top strengths in a different manner each day for a week. This experience led them to be much happier even six months later.

DISCOVERING YOUR CHARACTER STRENGTHS

You might be wondering what are character strengths and how are you supposed to know what yours are? Here are a few questions that might start to give you a sense of what your gifts are:

What am I really good at (that I love doing)?

What would my friends, colleagues, and family say that I am good at?

What do other people ask me to help them with?

Character strengths can include things like creativity, honesty, love of learning, curiosity, perseverance, bravery, kindness, etc. Rather usefully, these have been mapped out by the VIA Institute into 24 cross-culturally valid signature strengths. These qualities have then been divided into 6 distinct groups. As you read through the groups and signature strengths below notice which ones really resonate with you.

1) Wisdom and Knowledge which includes these qualities: **Creativity** (originality and ingenuity), **Curiosity** (interest, novelty-seeking, open-ness to experience), **Judgment** (critical thinking), **Love of Learning** (the passion for systematically expanding what one knows), **Perspective** (wisdom).

2) Courage which includes these qualities: **Bravery** (valor), **Perseverance** (persistence and industriousness), **Honesty** (authenticity and integrity), **Zest** (vitality, enthusiasm, energy and vigor).

3) Humanity which includes these qualities: **Love** (valuing close relationships and being close to people), **Kindness** (generosity, care, compassion), **Social Intelligence** (emotional intelligence and personal intelligence).

4) Justice which includes these qualities: **Teamwork** (citizenship, loyalty, social responsibility), **Fairness** and also **Leadership.**

5) Temperance (a word that is rarely used these days but refers to strengths that protect against excess). In this group are these qualities: **Prudence** (being careful about one's choices), **Forgiveness, Humility** and **Self-Regulation** (self-control).

6) Transcendence which includes these qualities: **Appreciation of Beauty and Excellence** (awe, wonder), **Gratitude** (appreciation), **Hope** (optimism, future-orientation), **Humor** (playfulness), **Spirituality** (faith, purpose).

A character strength is potentially a bit like your superpower and is worth recognizing and using as such because doing so will enable you to be much happier and more effective in the world. So what are your superpowers?

OK, that can be a tricky question to answer. *It can sometimes be difficult to be clear about which are the qualities that you actually have rather than the ones you think that you have or that you should have or would like to have.* Luckily, the VIA institute has created a free online survey where you can find out exactly what your personal character strengths (or superpowers) are. It only takes 10-15 minutes to complete, so I suggest that you take the survey now to get greater clarity.

http://www.viacharacter.org/www/Character-Strengths-Survey

USING THE SURVEY RESULTS

On completion of the VIA survey, you will instantly be able to download the results. It is possible to then pay for detailed reports with more information about these characteristics and how you could use this personal information, however, for the purpose of this exercise it is not necessary.

The most important information for you is what your top seven qualities are. By clarifying what your innate strengths are you will be able to understand yourself in a new and valuable way. You will also be able to start consciously using these attributes more effectively in many areas of your life to great effect.

THE SIGNATURE STRENGTHS EXERCISE

Choose one of your top seven character strengths and find a new way to use it at least once every day for a week. You may like to write in your journal how you used it each day.

You can then choose another one of your top characteristics on another week to practice. Repeat this exercise whenever you are looking for more inspiration and happiness in your life.

That's it! If you have the "My Happiness Journal" workbook that was designed to be used with this book, you will find it laid out for you to accomplish in an easy way. It is a very simple thing to do but it can be very powerful and is certainly an enjoyable experience and exploration.

WANT TO LEARN MORE ABOUT CHARACTER STRENGTHS?

Apart from the VIA Institute's amazing work, there is actually a "Character Strengths Day" organized every year which has been created to bring this wisdom and understanding to the greater general public as well as to schools. It is incredibly valuable to work with our strengths and it can improve our lives immensely.

For more information and inspiration, the Let It Ripple website provides some great resources about character strengths that you can download at any time. Find out more here:

http://www.letitripple.org/character_day

***

You will find the "My Happiness Journal" really useful for going exploring your character strengths in greater depth as it has sections in it for recording them and working with them over time. When you claim your happiness toolkit, you will be sent a coupon code to get the journal at a reduced price. To get your happiness toolkit go to the Reader Bonus Materials.

CHAPTER 5. EXERCISE, DIET AND SLEEP

"The groundwork of all happiness is health." – Leigh Hunt

It is worth noting that not only does being healthier have a positive emotional impact on us but also that happier people are less prone to illness and more able to recover from diseases and surgery.

Hopefully, most of us know that eating healthily, regularly exercising and sleeping well are good for our physical bodies. But how well do we actually follow this advice? For some of us, it can be confusing to know exactly how we can best do this and adopt new healthier habits. In this chapter, I hope to make this shift easier for you to understand and do.

If you have already tried taking greater care of your physical body in this way for a while you will also have discovered that you feel much better emotionally and mentally too.

THE VALUE OF REGULAR EXERCISE

Our distant ancestors used their bodies to do lots of physical activities such as hunting, gathering, farming, building, etc. It has been estimated that on average they would have walked 8 miles per day. Our bodies evolved not only to be able to cope with lots of physical activity but also to function more effectively when we are very active. This then is a massive challenge for our modern "seat-orientated" society – we sit for breakfast, sit in the car/bus/train to commute, sit at work then sit in front of the TV at night to recover from the stress and sitting that we have been doing all day!

As a result, the general population's health has deteriorated in many ways. But it is not just our physical health that is affected by the lack of movement and exercise. Our emotional and mental health are deeply affected by the ways that we use (or do not use) our bodies too. Regular exercise has been found to improve our brain's performance whilst also reducing cognitive decline and the development of Alzheimers!

> *"Walk to be healthy, walk to be happy."*
> – Charles Dickens

When we do regular exercise our bodies release endorphins, seroto-nin, norepinephrine and dopamine (happy hormones and neurotransmitters) that make us feel great afterward. Exercise also reduces our stress and anxiety levels, gives us a sense of self-mastery and motivation as well as elevating our mood and our potential to be more productive.

There have been some fascinating studies that have looked at the im-pact of exercise on people who have been diagnosed as clinically depressed. In these studies, they compared the effects of exercise to the effects of the most (over) prescribed anti-depressant drugs on the market. What was particularly remarkable was that exercise was shown to be just as effective as the drugs were in the short-term yet in the long-term exercise was actually found to be *more* effective as the positive benefits lasted much longer!

EXERCISE FOR YOU

"Does running late count as exercise?" – Anon.

You may be wondering what particular exercise program I am going to suggest that you do and whether you will be able to do it or even whether you will want to do it.

Well, I am actually going to suggest that you do whatever physical ac-tivity that you would really enjoy doing – walking, running, dancing, playing Frisbee, rebounding, tennis, etc. It does not matter too much what you do as long as you are getting some form of effective physical exercise that raises your heart rate. If it is an activity that you love or enjoy you are far more likely to maintain the motivation and inspira-tion to do it regularly.

In the experiments that looked at the impact of doing exercise on depressed people, the requirement was to exercise for 30 minutes 3 times per week. Exercising at least 3 times per week is probably a good baseline. However, I have also seen that doing shorter workouts such as a fast 20-minute walk or even the practice of Tabatas can be very effective too. (Tabatas are intense 4-minute workouts that consist of 8 x 20-second rounds of full power exercise interspersed by 10-second rests. You can get some great phone, kindle and computer Tabata apps that make this practice easy.)

Another couple of helpful tips are: do not try to do too much to start with (e.g. start with a daily 4-minute Tabata or 20 minutes of exercise 3 x per week and increase this when and if you feel inspired to). If you are not used to exercising and feel unfit, then walking can be a great place to begin. Doing an exercise activity with friends such as a sport or other shared experience can make it more fun and therefore more inspiring for you to do and to keep up. You might also like to combine the experience with great music or an interesting audio book which can make your exercise more enjoyable, easier and potentially a way to learn something new at the same time.

DANCE

I am going to make a brief mention about the value of dancing because it has been a fundamental means of expression and connection for humans throughout history. I know that there will be many people who read this book who do not see themselves as dancers or even consider dance as a form of exercise (and there will be many who love to dance and perhaps just see it as something that they really enjoy). However, when I speak about dance in this context, I am not referring to particular formal dance styles and moves, or looking cool or even being a good dancer but to our body's natural capacity for enjoyment through movement inspired by music. Have you ever seen a group of small children reacting to music, perhaps at a kids' party? They probably jumped, jiggled, wiggled, stomped and bounced in delight. It wasn't about looking good or even necessarily being in time with the rhythm; it was just about expressing fun.

The saying "to jump up and down with joy" is an acknowledgment of the natural urges that our bodies have to express various types of emotion through movement. In fact, you will discover in Chapter 8 "Using Your Physiology," how facial expressions, standing postures, and physical movements can all manifest different emotional responses within your body and mind.

Dance invokes happiness and happiness inspires dance.

Throughout my travels around the world and particularly my time spent with groups of people still living in fairly traditional ways, it was very normal to find that for the vast majority of these people dance was an important and central part of their cultures. It was also an important way for groups to feel connected with one another and that sense of connection in our lives is also a very important key to happier living.

So, I encourage you to consider bringing dance into your life (even if it is behind closed doors when no one is looking). It can be a particularly valuable way of warming up for a workout or even as your whole exercise practice, especially as part of the jumpstart to joy morning ritual that you will learn about in Chapter 11. You could also use it as a way to celebrate and express your gratitude and joy – you will learn more about that in the form of the *happy dance* in Chapter 8!

HEALTHY EATING

This is a massive topic all in itself and having studied and taught about nutrition for over a decade, I am aware how complicated and confusing the subject can sometimes be. However as diet and our resultant health can have such an impact on our physical and emotional well-being, I am going to offer you a very, *very* simple guide to how to eat much more healthily.

- Eat lots of fresh vegetables and some fruit.

- Eat less meat.

- Avoid sugar and stimulants.

- Reduce wheat products and carbohydrates.

- Consume good fats in your diet – especially oily fish*. (Other sources of good oils: flax seed oil, walnut oil, coconut oil, hemp seed oil, olive oil, avocado oil, nuts and seeds.)

* One word of caution; although oily fish provide the most effective form of bioavailable omega-3s with DHA and EPA, they can also be contaminated with the heavy metals, pesticides and industrial chemicals that humanity has polluted the sea with. It is, therefore, best to only eat fish that are at the lower end of the food predator pyramid due to the fact that as small species are eaten by larger ones, contaminants are accumulated and concentrated. The best fish in this regard would be sardines, mackerel and salmon. Examples of the type of fish to avoid would be shark, tuna, and swordfish.

- Eat foods in or close to their natural state. (If you really want to eat some processed type foods, then you could try to process/make them yourself.)

- Do not eat foods that make you feel tired, sick, lousy or guilty (either during or afterward.)

N.B. It can also be useful to take supplements that will help you to reach optimal health and raise your mood. Deficiencies in omega-3s, B vitamins and vitamin D have all been found to be associated with depression and other mental/emotional disorders. So supplementing a healthy diet with these can be really helpful for supporting anyone to elevate their mood. (When choosing omega-3 fish oil supplements take 2-4g per day and make sure that they are guaranteed to be free from toxic contaminants!)

That's it. You might be quite shocked at how much healthier and more energized you feel after following these dietary principles for even just a few weeks.

AN EXERCISE TO OVERCOME EMOTIONAL EATING

It is worth me pointing out that some eating behaviors are related to emotional suppression and are therefore addictive eating patterns. We can consume food as a way of changing a set of feelings or a state that we do not like. Having supported thousands of people to fast, I have seen that a very large percentage of us use foods in this way without being aware of it at all.

If you recognize that you might be addicted to certain foods or ways of eating, then I recommend that whenever you feel that overwhelming urge to eat those foods or eat in that way, you use the following strategy.

OVERCOMING EMOTIONAL EATING

Stop (for my own amusement, I am tempted just to say "stop" and end there but for an approach that will be more practical for most people, I will offer some further suggestions) **and take 4 conscious breaths, then ask yourself what you are feeling. If you have a journal or note app on your phone, make a note of your feelings. This can be very insightful and can also allow and inspire you to take effective actions to remedy any situations in your life that are not working for you.**

At this point, if you have the time and space, it can be really helpful to use movement to change your state – try going for a walk or run, exercising for 5 minutes or even having a dance, if you really want that feel-good factor.

Once you have become conscious of what might be going on for you and maybe had a chance to change your state through movement, you can then reassess whether you actually want to eat or not. You are likely to find that in many cases, you no longer have that "must eat it now" drive.

PROPER SLEEP

There is another vital requirement for living in an optimal state of physical, mental and emotional health and that is getting an adequate amount of good quality sleep. Improving your sleep can be an incredibly fast and easy way to raise your happiness set point.

I am going to write more about this particular area of better health than I have on either exercise or diet because, by comparison, there is relatively less information out there about the subject, many people are misinformed about it and most people have no idea how poor sleep can impact their emotional, mental and physical life or what factors influence the quality of sleep. Understanding the problems associated with poor sleep and committing to sleeping better is an easy way to improve your health and your happiness.

Sleep is a period of restoration and repair for the body as well as a time for the mind to process the day's events and file away memories.

Before the Industrial Revolution and the invention of the light bulb, humans generally slept 7.5-12 hours per night (bizarrely, in many places around the world, this was apparently in 2 parts with a 1-2 hour break in between) as well as having a mid-afternoon nap. After this, the new concept of "time is money" and an ever increasing push for doing more has meant that we have constantly reduced our hours of sleep. Today, the average American sleeps for 6.5 hours each night which is 20% less than they slept just 30 years ago!

Our bodies are not designed to work in this way. As one of the foremost sleep specialists, Dr. Kirk Parsley said, *"Our bodies aren't machines. Our cells have embedded clocks in them that refuse to adapt to our desire to push through our need for sleep."*

What is quite shocking is that numerous studies have found that chronic sleep deprivation increases our risk of cancer, heart attacks, strokes, diabetes, obesity, depression, accidents, and suicide! It also reduces our performance levels, creativity, mental capacity and our ability to learn and retain new information.

The opposite side of this equation is that adequate, good quality sleep at night and even short power naps in the day have a powerful positive effect on our physical, emotional and mental health and capacity. Sleeping well, naturally, reduces the risk of suffering from all of the formerly mentioned illnesses.

It has been known for quite a while that the optimal amount of sleep is between 6 and 8 hours. Sleeping much longer than 8 hours per night on a regular basis has actually been found to be detrimental to health.

More recently, the relevance of the circadian rhythms within which we sleep have been shown to be incredibly important. We sleep in 90-minute cycles and whenever we awaken at the completion of one, we actually feel much more refreshed and rejuvenated than had we woken in the middle of one. This means waking after 6 or 7.5 hours' (or sometimes 9 hours) sleep is better for you than sleeping for 6.5, 7, 8 or 8.5 hours of sleep. Try to sleep in a multiple of 90-minutes at night; 7.5 hours is optimal (and 6 hours occasionally is fine.)

Going to sleep earlier than you are used to (unless you are already going to bed very early) can be really valuable. Even going to bed one hour or half an hour earlier can have a profound effect on your quality of sleep, your energy levels and how you feel. There is an old naturo-pathic adage that says that every hour before midnight that you sleep is worth two hours of sleep after midnight. If you are going to bed early and have a more than adequate amount of sleep then I recom-mend that you try waking up an hour or two earlier.

"Early to bed and early to rise makes a man healthy, wealthy and wise."
– Anon.

As you adjust your sleeping hours to a more effective amount, it is also helpful to consistently go to bed and wake up at roughly the same time. Creating such a pattern enables your body to more readily drop straight into a deep sleep.

In my own experience changing my sleep patterns to earlier to bed and earlier to rise (despite my inner rebel that wanted to stay up later because I am a grown up now), as well as sleeping for either 6 or 7.5 hours at night, in line with my circadian cycles, has had a hugely positive impact on my life in terms of feeling fully rested and nourished. This is, of course, a much better place from which to enjoy life and be happier.

THE QUALITY OF SLEEP

As well as the length and timing of sleep, the quality of your sleep is very important. The factors that impact the quality of your sleep are to do with light, sound, temperature and comfort.

In regards to light, it is very important to make your environment as similar to the natural world's light levels as possible i.e. midday light should be blue/white, evening light should fade into the yellow spectrum, night-time should be completely dark.

NAPPING

It turns out that we are actually designed to sleep twice per day, by having a long sleep at night as well as a shorter midday sleep. This is how humans have lived for the majority of their existence and it is programmed into our genes.

I often assumed that many of the people who came to see me for health issues that included afternoon tiredness were suffering from some type of food intolerance until I began looking at the research into napping. I now realize that although this is certainly true for some people, for many others it is more likely to be a reflection of their not having adequate sleep at night and our inherent human design that works optimally when we nap in the day as well.

Sara C. Mednick, Ph.D., a researcher at the Salk Institute and the leading authority on the study of the nap, has found that regular napping increases alertness, boosts creativity, reduces stress, improves perception, stamina, motor skills, and accuracy, enhances your sex life, helps you make better decisions, keeps you looking younger, aids in weight loss, reduces the risk of heart attack, elevates your mood, and strengthens memory – wow!

So make sure that you are getting enough good sleep to nourish your body and mind – because this will in turn support you in your quest for and experience of greater happiness.

LEARN MORE ABOUT HOW TO IMPROVE YOUR SLEEP

If you would like to discover how to upgrade the quality of your sleep, I have included a bonus chapter at the end of the book entitled How to Improve Your Sleep. This goes into the topic in greater detail and will be very useful for you to explore if you are aware that you are not sleeping as well as you possibly could be. It will also enable you to improve your capacity to be productive, creative and alert in the daytime.

CHAPTER 6. RANDOM ACTS OF KINDNESS

"Remember that the happiest people are not those getting more, but those giving more." – H. Jackson Brown Jnr.

The power and beauty of kindness is that it is done for its own sake and from a place of compassion or sometimes from a sense of connection and playfulness. Kind acts are not done in repayment for some previous action, rather, they are done because we want other humans, (sometimes people who we do not even know), to suffer less and to experience relief or happiness.

These altruistic actions end up being valuable for everyone involved – the giver, the receiver and anyone who was fortunate to witness the act!

Studies of the impact of reaching out to help others have shown that altruism leads to reduced depression, increased happiness, more energy, a calmer mind, greater self-worth and even a kind of euphoria.

Being generous has also been shown to help people thrive in their businesses and careers. Professor Andrew Grant who wrote *Give and Take: Why Helping Others Drives Our Success,* noticed that highly successful people tend to be givers – people who give of themselves with no strings attached.

"Being radically generous is not just a warm and fuzzy feeling. It's a way of being that can cause you to be wildly successful."
– John Ruhlin (Gift-ology)

In her book *The How of Happiness*, Sonya Lyubomirsky describes an experiment where participants did 5 acts of conscious kindness during one day. They were found to be much happier and to experience more positive emotions afterward than control groups and they also continued to do so for an unexpectedly long period of time.

There has been much research that has shown that kindness leads to much better health. In one study, doing regular volunteer work in a compassionate way was shown to increase life expectancy and overall vitality (*James House, University of Michigan*). In another study, participants were found to have increased levels of antibodies after just watching a documentary about Mother Teresa (*David McClelland, Harvard University*).

"The secret to living is giving." – Tony Robbins

It would seem that humans are actually wired to be compassionate. This may be because we evolved as a species that functioned best when its members were constantly supportive of each other. We are naturally heart-full and caring beings when we are in our inherant state.

COMPASSION

"If you want others to be happy, practice compassion. If you want to be happy, practice compassion." – The Dalai Lama

Committing conscious acts of kindness enables us to enter a compassionate state of being. To do this we have to allow ourselves to feel our connection with other people's struggles and suffering and then be inspired to alleviate it in some way.

The Dalai Lama has stated that *"genuine compassion is based on the rationale that all human beings have an innate desire to be happy and overcome suffering. Once we recognize the commonality and connection that we have with everyone else, we naturally generate love and compassion."*

Compassion is a cornerstone of all religions and also is found as a deeply important part of many traditional tribal ways of living. A beautiful example of this would be the teachings of "the giveaway" in native North American traditions, where the giving of useful gifts, food, and possessions to other members of one's tribe who were in need was seen as virtuous and totally necessary for the tribe's survival. I once heard it said that you could often tell who a tribal chief was because he had the least possessions having given so much away for the betterment of his people. How different our world would be today if that was how we all lived!

GENEROSITY

Another aspect of kindness and compassion is generosity. We can be generous on many levels not just in the obvious monetary way but also it could be with our time, possessions, care or wisdom. This generous behavior may be direct with the beneficiary or indirect in such forms as charitable giving.

Interestingly, several psychology experiments have shown that we experience longer lasting joy and pleasure when we spend money on others or doing things with others than when we spend it purely on ourselves. This brings an interesting twist to the idea that money cannot buy you lasting happiness – it seems that sometimes it can when you spend it on other people!

ELEVATION

Fascinatingly, it is not just the person who receives an act of kindness nor just the person who acts altruistically who receive the benefits of such caring behavior. People who witness these acts are also positively impacted.

The adjacent ripple effect of acts of kindness has been termed "Elevation." This is the experience of uplifting positive thoughts and feelings that any observer of acts of kindness has. I will speak a bit more about this in the Butterfly Effect chapter later but for now, just know that whenever you commit acts of kindness, the effects can be unexpectedly far-reaching.

In a novel experiment by researcher Alice Isen, gratitude was shown to increase kindness. She left coins in phone booths and then pretended to accidently drop her paperwork outside the phone booth just after the lucky recipient of the free phone money emerged from the booth. She found that there was a much higher chance that the people who had received money would go out of their way to help her, whilst those who had not discovered the free money were much less likely to assist her. It would seem that gratitude inspires us to be more trusting that we are part of a benevolent universe, so much so, that we are inspired to be more kind and helpful.

Richard Layard found in his research for the book *Happiness: lessons from a new science,* that people are now half as likely to trust other people as they were just 50 years ago. Increasing trust through consciously being kind is certainly a valuable reversal of direction for our societies to move in. The practice of committing random acts of kindness is just one such great way of doing just that.

THE RANDOM ACTS OF KINDNESS EXERCISE

A simple way to do this is to choose one day where you will commit to doing 5 acts of conscious kindness. (Conscious meaning that you have clearly decided to do something for the benefit of someone else beforehand and not just something that later in the day you can look back on in retrospect and decide that it could be counted as one of your acts.) These acts should be done purely for someone else's benefit and not for any reward or praise.

Alternatively, you could try this exercise: do at least one random act of kindness every day (or as many times per week as feels easy for you to start with), for one or two weeks. Be aware of how you felt afterward and keep a record of it. At the end of the week look back through your journal and reflect on how these experiences made you and the people who might have been involved feel. You may find that you are inspired to continue to do this practice just because it felt so great!

If you are short on ideas of what you could do then I suggest that you check out the Random Acts of Kindness website that has a section that is full of brilliant and inspired ideas:

www.randomactsofkindness.org/kindness-ideas

PAYING IT FORWARDS

I want to share the wonderful concept of *paying it forwards* with you so that recipients of your kind acts do not end up feeling uncomfortably indebted and the energy of generosity can keep flowing.

In his book *Influence: The Psychology of Persuasion,* researcher Robert Cialdini Ph.D. states that we are all bound by a rule of reciprocation, that is "that we should try to repay, in kind, what another person has provided us." This obligation to repay favors that we have received is deeply woven into our human psyche because it has been so necessary for the successful evolution of human society. Reciprocal generosity enabled us to share food and skills, co-operate, work together and build trust. However, in recent years, this automatic response has been misused by the advertising and marketing industry to manipulate us into buying various goods and services. As such, we have lost much trust in others and can often be unconsciously wary about why people might help us or the debt that we may be obliged to repay.

Acting from the perspective of paying it forwards allows the recipients of our kindness to just accept and appreciate the experience and probably to be inspired to act in a more generous and kind way themselves, in the future.

I first came across this way of being generous in 1986 in Greece. I was traveling around Europe in a VW camper van with my school friend, Gareth. We were working in agricultural greenhouses on the island of Crete, for shockingly low wages and surviving on a very tight budget. One day we were invited to dinner at a restaurant by an older traveler who Gareth had met that day. I was rather surprised that a complete stranger had offered to take us out to a restaurant and I expressed my curiosity about his generosity. He responded that he had also had a time when he was struggling and lacking money when he was first traveling, so he knew what it was like. At that time, several people had helped him, asking for nothing in return other than that he could return the favor to someone else in need at some point in the future. He was happy to help us and just invited us to *pay it forwards* by supporting others in the future.

Since that time, I have found myself on many occasions in situations where I was able to happily help people. I have a sense of myself being part of a chain of goodwill and kind-heartedness that is rippling outwards. I am often intrigued when I consider what positive and generous actions may occur elsewhere for others, as a result of the kindness that I have shown. Connecting with others in this way can be a great reminder that we are all part of one large human family.

Paying It Forwards Card

You have just received a kindness from someone - possibly even a complete stranger! This was offered from a place of generosity & heartfulness, without any expectation or obligation that you should return the favor in any way.

If, however, you have an opportunity in the future to be kind or help another member of your human family, remember that it can be done in this way. Feel free to pass this card onto them at the time so that they might also be inspired to keep the kindness rippling outwards. This is the principle behind "paying it forwards." It is an amazing way to spread happiness.

www.choosing-happier.com

To be able to give from the paying it forwards perspective successfully it may be necessary to explain the concept to the receiver of your generosity. To make this easier, I have actually designed some simple business type cards that explain the concept (you will find them in the happiness toolkit). Should you wish to carry out some random acts of kindness for strangers in this way, you can just give them a card or leave it where they will find it, after doing your good deed.

The concept of paying it forwards actually became popularized by the Hollywood film "Pay it Forward," in 2000. It is perhaps a little cheesy at the end but it does exemplify how this attitude can multiply outwards.

"Kindness in words creates confidence. Kindness in thinking creates profoundness. Kindness in giving creates love." – Lao Tzu

---

CHARITABLE SUPPORT

Today, we are able to support people at a distance more easily than ever before. Sometimes the people or causes who could really benefit from our support are far away from where we live. Also, we may not have the time, skills or capacity to help them. Thankfully, if we are able, we can still help by donating financially to these causes which will not only be beneficial for them, it will also expand our happiness.

You may even find it really valuable to tune in to which people or causes you are most concerned about and become a passionate advocate for them. If you have not considered this before, you might find asking this question really helpful:

If I had $10 million to donate to noble causes, who would I give it to?

Once you are clear what your cause is, do not be afraid to let your friends, family and colleagues know about it – they may be inspired to support it too or else to put energy into championing a cause that they really believe in.

ESCALATING THE POWER OF KINDNESS

"The best way to find yourself is to lose yourself in the service of others."
– Gandhi

If you also use your innate strengths (the ones that you discovered by taking the VIA questionnaire), to be effective and compassionate within a cause that you care about, you will increase the impact of your kindness.

Using your signature strengths engenders more happiness and the potential for dropping into the *flow state* (that state of timeless focus, connection and being authentically oneself) which leads to the second level of happiness, *engagement* (as categorized by Martin Seligman). Being in service to a greater good, to a cause that you personally feel is really important will then enable you to move into the third category of happiness, *the meaningful life* which is by far the most impactful and long-lasting form of happiness.

So I encourage you to get in touch with what is really important to you (see the chapter on purpose) and find a way to use your character strengths to be kind, helpful and valuable in service of that noble cause.

To add yet another layer of happiness-inducing potentiality to this experience you could also find a way to do this in conjunction with your friends, family or social network, for as you will learn in the next chapter, having strong social relationships is incredibly important for living more happily.

"The wise man does not lay up his own treasures. The more he gives to others, the more he has for his own." – Lao Tzu

A POWERFUL TOOL FOR CHANGE

Hopefully, you can see how powerful these practices are. Practicing kindness helps us to cultivate our compassion and to become happier and kinder. Developing compassion inspires us to be kind both to ourselves and others. As we carry out acts of caring in the world we make other people's lives easier and bring them happiness. At the same time, anyone who witnesses our compassionate behavior will be positively impacted too. Both those who receive kindness and those who witness it are much more likely to act in kind ways to other people that they know or meet. Those future recipients of kindness are in turn likely to be kind to others, creating a ripple of kind-heartedness that could reach unexpectedly far. (I will look at this in more detail later in Chapter 18 "The Butterfly Effect".) As such being kind is not only great for you but has the potential of creating a revolution of the heart that could actually have an impressive and far reaching positive impact in the world.

***

If you are inspired by some of these ideas I recommend that you download the happiness toolkit if you have not already done so. It includes a template for the Pay It Forwards cards to print and use. To get your happiness toolkit go to the Reader Bonus Materials.

CHAPTER 7. SOCIAL CONNECTION

"Friendship improves happiness and abates misery, by the doubling of our joy and the dividing of our grief."
– Marcus Tullius Cicero (106-43 BC)

The strength of our social relationships is one of the strongest indicators for our levels of happiness and resilience in the face of challenging experiences.

As I mentioned at the beginning of this book, when people who were found to be consistently happy were studied for the "Very Happy People" research project at the University of Illinois, they found that the only thing that the top 10% of happy people had in common was the fact that they all had strong social relationships. Remarkably this was much more important than their wealth, health, race, gender, age, religious beliefs, social background, or the even the amount of challenging or good experiences in their lives.

In our development as a species, we have almost always worked and lived in communities. This is one of the factors that allowed us to survive and thrive. In traditional settings, it was rare for individuals to spend extended periods of time surviving on their own. We function better and are more resilient and strong when working and living as a group.

Understanding how our modern world appears from that more traditional perspective can also provide unexpected insights. On several occasions when speaking with people who were still living in fairly traditional societies I was asked about why people live in such a lonely way in the West. To people who live with the joy and support that come from real communal connection, our way of living seems very bizarre and unnatural.

In the modern Western world, we have become absorbed in the ideal of the independent individual who achieves everything on their own.

However, this is not a truthful view of reality or an effective or healthy way to live. It is not truthful because we are actually far, far away from being independent. Unless you are from one of the rare tribes in the Amazon jungle who has not come into contact with the modern world, then you are surrounded by modern material possessions and food that you did not catch, hunt, forage or grow yourself. Of course, if you were one of those indigenous peoples, you would be unlikely to be reading this book right now and probably wouldn't need to either!

"Everything that is in the heavens, on earth, and under the earth is penetrated with con-nectedness, penetrated with relatedness."
– Hildegard von Bingen

Have you ever stopped to consider how many people have taken part in the process of getting these things to you in their present form? For example, I have my favorite thermos cup on my desk next to me, so that I can sip hot tea as I write. It is made of steel. The iron ore from which it originated would have been mined far away, transformed into steel at a distant steel plant, molded into its present shape in a factory, painted pale blue in that factory, then packaged and sent to the shop from which it was bought. Designers or engineers would be involved with each creative stage of the process – the cup's shape, its logo, and the packaging. Each part of this process required people to be working in the various mines, plants and factories as well as for the transport between the different stages. The transport required fuel and there-fore everyone and everything that is necessary to make oil into an accessible form of energy, must also be considered.

The amount of people and resources that have been required to pro-duce this one item is almost incomprehensible. I am barely scratching the surface in the above description! It is just a cup for me to drink hot liquid from but actually I have literally thousands of people to be grateful to for its very existence.

We may never have considered it before but we are not at all independent, rather we are extremely interdependent in the modern world.

We are also recognizing how inter-related we are. Genetic based genealogy studies have shown how much our ancestors traveled and mixed around the planet and therefore, how closely related we all are. Our present day divisions by country borders, cultures or languages are a very poor reflection of our common ancestral connections.

This greater sense of being interconnected has also been amplified by our more recent achievements in technology and our explorations into space. The ease of instant communication to people around the world via the Internet and profound impact of being able to observe our planet from space have presented humanity with an exciting new level of self-awareness – the recognition that we are all part of one ginormous extended family.

One of the downsides of trying to live completely independently is that when we attempt to do everything on our own and we shun support and help from others we are in fact much less effective, productive, happy, healthy or resilient. When we have a strong social support system (in the form of friends, partners, spouses, colleagues) we greatly increase the intellectual, emotional and physical resources that enable us to effectively respond to any situation. In challenging times we are able to share our thoughts and get feedback and support that make it easier to find solutions.

"No two minds ever come together without,
thereby, creating a third, invisible, intangible
force which may be likened to a third mind."
– Napoleon Hill

We can also be uplifted by our friends who can appreciate and celebrate us and our achievements. These attributes all lead to us being happier and thereby being more successful and fulfilled in nearly every aspect of life.

THE HARVARD STUDY OF ADULT DEVELOPMENT

This incredible ongoing study by Harvard university which began in 1938, was designed to discover what keeps us healthy and happy. They chose 472 men and followed them through their lives, asking them questions every 2 years, checking their medical records and interviewing them, their wives and children, (in fact, many of their wives are now part of the study too). As a result, they have managed to get a fascinating snapshot of the impact of the way that we live on our physical and emotional health. The main lessons that can be learned from this inquiry are:

1) Good social connections and relationships keep us happier and healthier – conversely, loneliness is toxic for us.

2) It is the quality of your close relationships that matters most.

3) Good relationships protect our bodies and our brains – memories are sharper for longer.

SOCIAL SUPPORT AND HEALTH

There have been lots of studies that have shown that a strong social support system results in much better physical health because it actually has a measurable impact on our cardiovascular, neuroendocrine and immune systems.

People in loving and happy relationships are far less likely to have heart attacks than unhappily married or single people. Also, a happily married person who does have a heart attack or heart bypass surgery will have 3-4 times better survival rates.

Good social connections also stimulate the release of oxytocin (a happy hormone) whilst lowering cortisol levels (a stress hormone).

Bizarrely it has been shown that social support has as much impact on our health and longevity as high blood pressure, smoking, obesity, and exercise!

THE VALUE OF TOUCH

"A hug is like a boomerang – you get it back right away."
– Bill Keane

Touch is another aspect of human relating that has a great impact on us. Whenever we have positive physical contact with another person our body releases oxytocin – the feel-good hormone. This is no doubt an evolutionary development because having such a response enabled us to bond and form connections with others around us so that we were encouraged to work together as a group whose survival chances were better. Positive touch also reduces the amount of stress hormones in the body.

In laboratories, it has been found that young animals that are regularly petted and stroked develop larger brains, stronger bones, and muscles as well as better immune systems than animals that are deprived of such touch.

It has also been found that babies or children who were deprived of physical touch did not develop normally, were prone to more illness and in some cases, they actually died due to the lack of that basic connection. That need does not dissipate with age.

Physical touch can be very beneficial to our health and emotional well-being. At the same time, lack of touch can be detrimental. In her book *Touch*, Tiffany Fields talks about how the symptoms of children diagnosed with ADHD were reduced when given regular massages. Similarly, teenagers prone to aggressive behavior were also found to experience less anxiety and aggressiveness after receiving regular massage treatments.

How quickly touch impacts us can be shown by an observation that has been made in intensive care units where coronary heart patients with fluttering heartbeats will suddenly have calmer and more regular heart rhythms when a nurse holds their hand to take their pulse.

It is great to recognize that even simple actions such as shaking hands with a stranger or hugging friends will have a valuable impact on your health and well-being as well as on theirs.

Having good friends and close family members can be very helpful to your emotional and mental balance but hopefully, as you can see, having a positive physical connection with them (and not just a text, Facebook or email connection) is an invaluable part of this.

MULTI-LEVEL HAPPINESS

Greater happiness in one person inspires more happiness in others. You may already be realizing that when we attempt to become happier for ourselves we start to have an effect on others in our community and social circles too. The degree to which this happens can be quite surprising as you will discover in the Butterfly Effect chapter that looks at the ever expanding positive impact of a happier lifestyle on the people around us.

When developing and strengthening your social network you may find it useful to ponder these wise words:

"You are the average of the 5 people that you spend the most time with."
– Jim Rohn

It is always helpful to spend time with people who are of value to you, who perhaps uplift or inspire you or certainly who can be supportive. These are things that you also want to be doing for your friends of course but make sure that this is a mutual experience so that you all benefit and grow from your shared time together.

Apart from it just being nice, fun and inspirational for people to share time with us when we are happier, some of the previous exercises will also have a direct and valuable effect on them.

Verbally practicing appreciation by expressing to others what it is that you actually appreciate about them will make them feel seen and better about themselves. It may also make them aware of some of their character strengths and likable qualities which in turn will engender greater happiness.

> ### FRIENDS APPRECIATION EXERCISE
>
> **Contact a friend or family member. This could be by meeting up with them in person, skyping with them, writing them an email or even a real letter. Tell them what it is that you value, admire or appreciate about who they are or some things that they have done. This does not have to be a long descriptive list (although it could be). Sometimes just a brief expression of appreciation for one of their attributes is enough. Repeat this regularly for different people in your life.**

Another very powerful and valuable exercise to try is...

HONORING YOUR POSITIVE INFLUENCERS

It is always deeply moving to discover how we positively touch other people's lives. However, we rarely take the time to let those who have been really important in our lives know what an impact they had. Doing the following exercise is likely to stir up a profound amount of joy for both you and the people that you do this exercise with. (In fact, it may be one of the most profound moments of your life!)

> **Write a list of people who have had a profound positive impact on you and your life. They could be people that you are still close to or a school teacher or other figure from your past whose conduct, words, support or wisdom were really valuable to you and formative to your way of being.**

Choose one of them. Take time to really consider what it was about who they were and what they said or did that was so helpful and inspiring for you. Then write them a heartfelt letter sharing your appreciation and recognition of the positive impact that they have had in your life, including how it affects the way that you live now.

Once you have written the letter, take a moment to really tune in and feel how acknowledging this has made you feel inside. Now find a way to connect with this person and send, or better still, read the letter to them as soon as you are able to.

Not only will this experience feel incredibly powerful for you, it will also potentially be a very moving and meaningful experience for the receiver of this feedback and appreciation. In doing this exercise you will be increasing your sense of connection and support as well as spreading ripples of gratitude and happiness outwards in ever in-creasing circles. Over time, you can repeat this exercise for everyone who is on your list.

"Count your age by friends, not years. Count your life by smiles, not tears." — John Lennon

I once read a true story about an elderly man who, whilst attending a friend's funeral, was greatly saddened to hear all of the lovely stories that were being shared about his late friend. As a consequence, he decided to organize an early, pre-death gathering of his own friends and family, so that he would be able to witness, hear and receive all of those stories about himself whilst he was still alive. He and his friends had an amazing day.

It is for this reason that doing these exercises is particularly valuable because often, people do not express deep appreciation to others who have been really helpful or positively influential until it is too late.

Integrating Your Social Connections In Your Life

"Show me your friends and I will show you your future." – Unknown

It may seem like a bizarre concept to you if you already have a strong social network that you interrelate with regularly but scheduling social events and shared experiences can be essential if you have already given priority to work and other obligations in your life.

> Make a list of the most important people in your life – friends, family, and loved ones. You might also like to add acquaintances that you resonate with and would like to get to know better.
>
> Then make a list of ways to connect more effectively and regularly with these people. This could be sharing food, going out or doing things together, calling them on the phone, skyping with them or even emailing them (although face to face communication is always a much better option). Contact them and let them know that you would love to spend more time with them.
>
> Once you have some good ideas, schedule them in to make them real! In fact, I encourage you to schedule and set up your first connection today so that this process actually happens and gains momentum.

Making these lists and following up with writing letters and contacting people is made easier in the *My Happiness Journal.* You will be able to get this at a discounted price via the coupon in the Reader Bonus Materials.

To become connected to a community that is aligned with your desire to live in a happier way then I suggest that you join the private choosing happier online group. Here you can gain mutual support, encouragement, and connection. You can also put out a request for people to become your *joy buddies* (specific people who will encourage you on your journey to joy and vice versa – this personal level of accountability and support can be really valuable.)

Go to http://www.choosing-happier.com/community and ask to become a member.

If you would like to inspire your own community of friends and family about the information in this book, then right now, while you are reflecting on the value of your social connections, could also be a great moment to post a comment about it on your favorite social media platforms. You may find that you already have some great potential joy buddies in your close circle of friends, who might be keen to choose greater happiness by doing some of the books recommended exercises with you.

CHAPTER 8. USING YOUR PHYSIOLOGY

"The body isn't there simply to carry the head." – Candace Pert

Our moods and emotions have a massive impact on our physiology and our health. An emotional state will engender a set of responses in a person's body that we can all clearly recognize, such as changes in expression, posture and even breathing. For example, someone who is in a peaceful state is likely to have a slight smile, a relaxed body and slow breathing. Someone who is experiencing an anxious or fearful state might have wider eyes, an alert tension in their face and posture, as well as faster breathing. Someone who is feeling depressed might be looking downwards, have trouble making eye contact, have slumped shoulders and be breathing in a shallow way.

Whether we are observing such physiology from the outside when looking at another person or when we are observing it from the inside when we are in the middle of a particular emotion, the simple conclusion is that emotions create physical responses in our bodies.

Some of these physiological reactions can be responsible for long-term impacts on our health too. The spectrum of illnesses that people are more likely to be prone to frequently relates to their predominant emotional state. I illustrated this in the last chapter with the example of the reduced amount of heart attacks experienced by people who were in happy and loving relationships. Similarly, there are a collection of diseases that constantly stressed people are much more likely to be disposed to. So it can be fair to say that the long-term impact of the chemicals that our bodies produce, as well as the changes in our nervous systems that happen as a response to frequently maintaining certain emotional states, will directly affect our organ and body health.

"The chemicals that are running our body and our brain are the same chemicals that are in-

volved in emotion. And that says to me that . . .
we had better pay more attention to emotions
with respect to health."
– Candace Pert Ph.D.

THE SCIENCE OF EMOTIONS

You may be surprised to learn that there are specific chemicals that are released in our bodies when we are experiencing different emotions. The neuroscientist Candace Pert Ph.D. was one of the early researchers in this field and termed these chemicals "molecules of emotion." This is still a relatively new field of understanding but it has enabled us to have a much clearer picture of what is involved in an emotional state at the molecular level.

Certain thoughts, beliefs (ingrained, frequently repeated thoughts) and situations will trigger emotional responses in the body. That response begins in the hypothalamus in the brain which will start to manufacture specific peptides (small chain amino acid sequences) that correlate to that specific emotion. These neural peptides and neural hormones are then released via the pituitary gland into the bloodstream so that they flood the body. As they come into contact with trillions of cells they search for receptors on those cells with which they can dock. If they find the matching form of receptor on a cell's wall they will then trigger a cascade of biochemical events within the cell that changes how it behaves.

Candace Pert states that each cell is actually conscious. As the owner and sum of all of these trillions of conscious cells undergoing peptide induced internal changes, you will experience the phenomena as a feeling or emotional state.

Interestingly, the more that we trigger the release of particular peptides the more equivalent receptor sites will be created on new cells' walls over time. **This means that the more that we practice any**

emotion the easier it becomes for us to repeatedly experience that emotion!

THE MIND AND BODY ARE ONE

In our modern world, we are conditioned to perceive things with a scientific mindset. We dissect and separate things to help us analyze and understand them but this also leads to an inaccurate illusion of the world being made up of dependent, separate and distinct items. This is particularly misleading in the understanding of the human body. Just because we have different names for the various body parts and systems such as the muscles, tendons, bones, ligaments, fascia, blood, etc., it does not mean that they are completely independent of each other. They are actually functioning together as part of a whole organism. So too are the mind and body united.

The mind and body have an interdependent two-way relationship. Not only do our thoughts and emotions affect our bodies but our bodies affect our minds. This may seem obvious in such situations as when someone has been suffering from illness and pain which results in them being prone to depression, anxiety or some other negative mental state. However, the way that we breathe and fascinatingly, the physical postures that we adopt actually have a major impact on our physical bodies too.

THE PROFOUND IMPACT OF POSTURE

It is worth bearing in mind that about 60% of communication is non-verbal, i.e. it occurs through body language, facial expressions, and voice tone. Even though there is a great variety of ways of being, expressing and communicating in the myriad of cultures found on our planet, there is also a collection of universally understood ways of being and feeling that are expressed by particular postures. In fact, these seem to actually be transmitted through our genes as opposed to being learned. This was shown to be the case by Jessica Tracey who studied people who had been born blind and therefore would have been unable to learn postural or movement patterns by seeing them done by others. So for example, one of the innate expressions that she found common to all people was that of celebration, where it was automatic to raise the arms upwards in a vee shape and to have the chin slightly elevated.

A study called "Preparatory power posing affects performance and outcome in social evaluations" carried out by the Harvard Business School, was designed to assess if a student's performance would be affected by adopting certain postures before a mock interview. Half of the group were given specific power postures to pose in for 2 minutes before being interviewed (these were expansive with head held high, forehead facing up, shoulders back, chest out and arms loose by their sides or up in celebration). In the interview, they were graded on overall performance, hire-ability and speaker presence (passion and warmth). It was hypothesized that speaker presence would be the main factor that was improved but in actual fact, **the students who had adopted the power poses before their interviews scored much higher for all of their assessments**.

This experiment could have been understood as just looking at the impact of how postures can change our self-perception and how we emanate that to others. However, they decided to explore this phenomenon further to see if there were any actual physiological changes that occurred as a result of adopting various postures.

In a second experiment, another set of students were split into two groups. One group was instructed to adopt various power postures for five minutes, whilst the other group was instructed to adopt various disempowering postures (head lowered, shoulders down, arms crossed, hands tucked under legs) and then both groups were asked to gamble. The student's saliva was measured before and after these activities so that any hormonal changes could be assessed. The main hormones of interest were cortisol (which is related to stress, decreased immunity, increased blood pressure and poor long-term memory) and testosterone (which is associated with increased endurance, cognition and muscle mass, as well as feelings of confidence and power).

The fascinating results of the experiment showed that the "Power Posers" took 86% more risks and that their testosterone levels actually increased whilst their cortisol levels decreased! By comparison, those who had stood or sat in disempowering postures had decreased levels of testosterone and increased levels of cortisol, which led to them being much less effective.

According to Amy Cuddy, who was a member of the team that carried out these experiments, adopting power poses will increase abstract thinking abilities, pain threshold, risk-tolerance and levels of testosterone. Feeling powerful will make you more assertive, accept criticism more gracefully and turn you into a high performer.

"Basically, our bodies change our minds, our minds change our behaviors, and our behaviors change our outcomes."
– Amy Cuddy (Assistant Professor at Harvard Business School)

The clear insight of these experiments is that **just by changing our posture we can change the way that we feel, the way we think, the way that we act, the way that our body is working and the way that others perceive us. As such, we will change the results that we get.**

Just in case you would like to practice this at home or work, you should be aware that power poses can also be perceived as being socially aggressive, so it is worth remembering that it would be best to practice your poses *before* participating in a social interaction that you would like to feel more empowered in and not during it. Potentially, you can do these poses anywhere – right before leaving the house, just before taking an exam, in an elevator or even in the toilet. Just make sure you're alone so that you can really focus on the change in your body chemistry and not suddenly seem a bit weird to those around you.

Another way that you might want to integrate some of this postural wisdom into your life is through awareness of your sleeping and waking positions because it has been found that these will impact us in a similar way. About 40% of adults sleep in the fetal position (and twice as many women as men) but when we take up less space in such positions it encourages us to feel less capable. Counteracting this effect can be easily done by stretching or lying in an expansive position in bed for a couple of minutes before getting up. This will release hormones that increase energy and a sense of empowerment.

SMILING FOR JOY

"Sometimes your joy is the source of your smile but sometimes your smile can be the source of your joy." – Thich Nat Hanh

It is great to now know that we can change how we feel by choosing various postures to adopt, but the previously cited experiments were mainly focused on how to increase our sense of empowerment and performance and you might be asking how can this be applied to our pursuit of living in a happier state?

Well on one level, being more empowered, performing better and having a sense of greater control in our lives can certainly lead to more happiness but we can also stimulate the release of our happy hormones by acting in happy ways.

The simplest way to induce the release of feel-good hormones is by the act of smiling. We have an internal system called "facial feedback" which responds to the expressions that we make. Generally, we smile because we are happy, but studies have shown that we become happier when we smile. When our facial expression is a happy one our body starts to release joy hormones even when we are not initially feeling joyous.

When holding particular expressions it can actually be quite challenging to experience any of the non-corresponding emotions. Actually, the best way to understand this is by trying it, so...

Firstly, smile and then try thinking about negative or unhappy things. Then scrunch your face up in an angry or upset way and try to think positive or happy thoughts. Not so easy huh?

An interesting experiment was carried out by the German University of Mannheim, in 1988, to assess the impact of facial expressions without the potential for bias due to participants knowing what emotional response might be expected of them. To achieve this, an ingenious method was devised. Participants were asked to hold a pen in their mouths for a few minutes, either using their teeth (which activated the *zygomatic major* muscle used for smiling) or their lips (which would trigger the use of the *orbicularis oris* muscle that is used in frowning). They were then shown a cartoon and asked to evaluate how funny it was. The group who had unconsciously stimulated their smiling muscles by holding the pen between their teeth found the cartoon significantly funnier than the group who had unconsciously stimulated their frowning muscles by holding the pen with their lips.

The simple practice of smiling can have profound effects on people's emotional states and well-being. One study assessing the effectiveness of smiling on chronically depressed people found that just 5 minutes of smiling in a mirror every morning for 2 months was enough to clear their depression. This is because the act of smiling triggers our bodies into releasing dopamine, serotonin and endorphins which naturally fight off the negative effects of depression and stress whilst reducing the amounts of stress hormones (cortisol, epinephrine and dopac) in the system. This results in a more positive mental attitude, lower blood pressure and a greater level of relaxation.

Apart from stimulating the release of neuropeptides, smiling also increases the body's production of human growth hormone (HGH) by 87%. HGH is really valuable for boosting the immune system – as such, smiling can have a major positive impact on your health!

In fact, it would seem that those of us who smile more are actually likely to live longer. This was illustrated by a study at Michigan University of 230 baseball players which found that those who smiled widest and most genuinely on their original baseball card photos, lived 7 years longer than those who didn't smile!

The practice of smiling is also supported by the fact that people who see us smiling are very likely to smile back at us due to the mirror neurons that automatically mimic facial expressions and the enticing happiness hormones that we experience when we smile.

N.B. BOTOX CAN REDUCE YOUR CAPACITY TO FEEL!

As a quick aside, I think it is useful to be aware that Botox injections can have a greater impact than just reducing wrinkles. Because of the way that facial feedback works, if we inhibit the ability of certain facial muscles to function, then we also inhibit the ability of those muscles to send trigger messages to the brain, that would have enabled feeling the associated emotions.

Dr. Michael Lewis, who has studied this phenomenon, states *"Injections of Botulinum toxin A can affect the way we feel and even how we see the world."* This is particularly a problem when someone receives Botox for crow's feet lines (or laughter lines) at the sides of the eyes, as the associated muscles have an important function in genuine smiling. Dr. Lewis found that people who had such a treatment had significantly higher levels of depression because it *"reduced the strength of the smile and made people feel less happy."*

It is also relevant to consider the implications of not being able to fully smile on how people perceive and respond to someone who has had Botox treatment. When someone's smile includes their eyes it indicates that they are genuine and open in their expression. However, when the eyes are not involved, observers are likely to read their smile as being false or forced and as such may respond quite differently and in a more guarded way to that person.

Bearing in mind that botox treatments are used by many people to increase their happiness, it seems a tragedy that it can lead to them being less able to express or feel that emotion!

"Botox = early onset taxidermy!
I used to be afraid of making that joke in public
in case any of my audience had had Botox
therapy and were offended...
but then... how would I know?!?"
– Matt Harvey

FAKE IT TILL YOU BECOME IT!

The amazing thing about understanding the impact that our physiology has on us is that we do not have to be in a particular state to begin with to be able to mimic it and thereby feel it. The old adage "fake it till you make it" is actually true, although it is more accurate to say "fake it till you become it."

Here are three exercises that you can explore that will raise your happiness levels:

THE SMILING EXERCISE

Firstly, write down a list of all of the things that you can think of that make you smile. (This only needs to be done the first time that you do this exercise, although you may be inspired to add to this list over time.)

Now smile for 2-5 minutes. If it works for you, you can do this in front of a mirror but it's OK without one too. Become very aware and conscious of how you feel as you smile. How does the smile feel on your face and in your eyes? How does your chest and heart area feel when you smile?

Complete this exercise by pondering the following question: "I wonder what will make me smile today?"

STANDING CELEBRATION

Stand for 2 minutes with your feet apart, your arms reaching upwards in a v-shape and your head up. You might want to combine this with thinking about experiences that you feel proud of or that made you feel happy. Smile. If you feel inspired to bring movement into this posture you could jump up and down like you are celebrating some kind of personal victory.

THE HAPPY DANCE

Whenever something goes well for you, you achieve something that you wanted to or hear good news, then get up and do a silly and fun dance! Actually expressing your gratitude or happiness through physical movement will have a big impact on your physiology and increase your levels of joy. If you are inspired to practice your happy dance when you are around other people, it will probably make them happier too.

A great way to share your joy is by creating a video of yourself doing your happy dance. You could even have a friendly competition with friends and family to see who can make the funniest or most joyful happy dance video. Also, post it in the Choosing Happier Facebook page and use the #myhappydance hashtag to make it easy to find.

Enjoy and have fun with these exercises. They can be used at any time but are especially useful when done in the morning. If you feel courageous, you could even practice the smiling exercise as you commute to work or school on the bus, the train or in your car! You might be surprised what a positive impact you can have on people around you.

BONUS

If you would like to be inspired by some great happy dances, check out the Choosing Happier Facebook page.

https://www.facebook.com/choosinghappier

Also, feel free to post your own happy dances there.

***

You can start connecting with the impact of consciously smiling by using the smiling meditation that is included in the happiness toolkit that you have access to via the Reader Bonus Materials.

CHAPTER 9. CREATE A SUPPORTIVE ENVIRONMENT

"Environment is stronger than willpower."
– Yogananda Paramahansa

The environment within which we live and work can have a massive impact on how happy we are. To this end, it can be very valuable for you to set up your environment to increase your ease and enjoyment as much as possible.

> **When you think about your work or home environment how does it make you feel? If those feelings are not really positive, how could you change your living or working conditions in ways that would make them seem more inspiring and pleasant?**

Some possibilities and suggestions for improving your environment are:

- Play uplifting music in the background.

Reassess your music collection from the perspective of how different types of music make you feel and then consciously choose what you listen to in various circumstances. Create some music playlists that engender the following emotions and feelings: happiness, joy, tranquility, enthusiasm, energized, "go-for-it," etc. Then whenever you need to feel more of any of the above states, just listen to your playlist.

Tip: You may find it to be especially useful to listen to a happy tunes playlist early in the morning whilst you are getting ready for the day ahead of you.

- Beautify your work and living spaces with the use of color or decor so that they make you feel good.

Tip: If you have not considered the impact of color on your mood before then you may find this simple color guide helpful. Generally, lighter and brighter colors are more uplifting. Specifically, these colors can positively affect your mood in the following ways: Yellow is uplifting and inspires joy, optimism, and happiness (hence the cover of this book). Orange promotes a sense of fun, energy and warmth. Green creates a sense of hope, healing and relaxation. Blue inspires tranquility and focus. White creates a sense of purity and cleanliness. Naturally different shades and tones of these colors will affect you in varying ways, so it is helpful to really tune into yourself whilst looking at various color options to discover how they make you feel.

- Have pictures of loved ones or favorite places around you or on your computer.

- Make time in your life to be out in the beauty and simplicity of nature (this can be as simple as going outside for a 20-minute walk when the weather is good). Doing this every day can be invaluable.

- Watch inspiring and feel-good movies or shows.

- Keep your work and home spaces clutter free as this will support your mind to be clutter free too.

- Choose a ringtone for your phone that you really like or that makes you smile.

At the same time, it can also be useful to circumvent and change situations that are likely to increase negativity such as avoiding negative media, TV, and films. This may include the normal news sources, which as I noted previously, can present a very negative and biased view of reality. (By contrast, you might like to have a look at www.positive.news if you are interested in uplifting and inspirational stories!)

No doubt you can also come up with some great ideas for yourself that can really work for your environment. I encourage you to actually make some simple changes and see what a big difference they bring about.

DECLUTTER

"Sometimes the biggest gain in productive energy will come from cleaning the cobwebs, dealing with old business, and clearing the desks – cutting loose debris that's impeding forward motion." — David Allen

I would just like to say a little more about decluttering because I think that its value is often overlooked and underestimated.

One of the impacts of living in our modern consumer society is that most of us acquire and keep far more than we need. Many people have so many extraneous things that they do not have enough room for in their own homes, that they have to rent space in other buildings just to keep it. The self-storage industry is absolutely booming. In the USA it took 25 years for this new industry to build its first billion square feet of storage space, yet it only took another 8 years (between 1998 to 2005) to add its second billion square feet! In 2016, there were 78 square miles of under roof storage space in the USA!

When our environment is cluttered we often experience a subtle (or not so subtle) constant background sense of confusion, pressure or a feeling of being overwhelmed. Whether we pay attention to it or not, it is likely to impinge on our capacity to function optimally. The process of consciously decluttering can have a massive impact on our ability to live both more happily and more efficiently.

A friend of mine recently recommended that I learn about the KonMari technique of decluttering and home tidying when I mentioned that my living space was feeling too full. Marie Kondo, the creator of the KonMari techniques, is a petite Japanese woman who is totally inspired to help people to efficiently declutter. She has some great tips. As a result of following her simple suggestions, I managed to take 3 sacks of clothes to local charity shops (which seemed pretty impressive to me as this was probably about ¼ of all of my clothes!). Interestingly, after going through this process I felt happier and markedly lighter, as well as quite energized for a couple of weeks. I still feel more relaxed and spacious when at home.

Surprisingly I also noticed that it enabled me to release other things in my life that were no longer serving me. This was because the KonMari technique requires that we become very conscious and aware of how we feel inside ourselves in relation to our possessions and to find clarity about whether we should keep them or not. As such, we can then become much more aware of whether many aspects of our lives are serving us or not and therefore we can and should make a choice about these too.

If you would like to know more about the KonMarie technique, I would suggest reading her rather cutely named book *Spark Joy* or her other best seller book *The Life Changing Magic of Tidying Up*. (More information can be found in the Recommended Books section.)

"The objective of cleaning is not just to clean, but to feel happiness living within that environment." – Marie Kondo

---

David Allen, who wrote *Getting Things Done,* states that cleaning and clearing things up in our environment is a sure fire way to unleash more of our creative potential. This is because when we have any level of chaos and clutter around us, our brain's creative capacity is being used for storing a vague awareness of all that needs to be done and remembered instead of what it is best at. Therefore, creating a tidy environment and effective systems to organize our lives can enable us to become incredibly productive, innovative and imaginative.

Taking our excess possessions to charity shops and thrift stores is a really great practice because the money earned from their sale will be going to charitable causes and when more products are reused there is less environmental waste. So in a way, this is a means to practice kindness and generosity, which as we know, leads to more happiness.

N.B. It is worth considering the global issue of excessive waste production that is another main impact from living in a society based on (over) consumption. Our various means of waste disposal all have harmful environmental consequences, therefore, I encourage you to look at your management of possessions from a more conscious perspective and to use "**the 4 Rs.**" **Reduce** (the amount that you consume), **Repair** (items when you are able to prolong their lives), **Reuse** (yourself or allow others to reuse them by passing them on) and **Recycle** as much as possible.

If you have never considered this aspect of our consumption-based modern living then you might find it interesting to watch "The Story of Stuff" video which can be found on YouTube. The story of stuff organization have actually created a whole range of other thought-provoking and entertainingly presented short films at www.storyofstuff.org which I highly recommend watching.

FILTERING AND CHOOSING YOUR NEWS SOURCES

On the larger scale, we are greatly impacted by the news that we hear or see and as mentioned earlier our media has a high negativity bias. Many studies have found that when people receive a lot of negative news and information they are prone to becoming distrustful, anxious, cynical, isolated, and sometimes even paranoid.

As mentioned in the first chapter, our brains are wired to give a prominence to negative, fear-based information and they require at least 3 times more positive information to balance and overcome negative news. This is compounded by the fact that when our subconscious mind believes that we need to be fearful, it will signal our RAS (reticular activation system) to be on the lookout for even more negative news and information in our environment. This will inevitably result in a debilitating downward spiral.

The answer to this dilemma is two-fold; reduce the amount of negative news that you are willing to consume, whilst consciously choosing to receive more uplifting and inspiring news. Positive news has been found to lead to greater optimism, trust, hope, faith in humanity, connection, and self-efficacy (a person's belief in their ability to make a difference). Again, when you hear more positive news, your RAS will search for even more constructive information to support this affirmative view of reality.

Luckily, there is a move to encourage the proliferation of more positive news, called constructive journalism. This solutions-based journalistic approach is focused on redressing the imbalance in modern news coverage because of the valuable impact that such commentary can have on individuals and society as a whole. It does not ignore negative news but focuses on reporting more optimistic stories so that there is a balance.

To begin accessing more inspiring news sources you might be interested in looking up the newspaper and website called Positive News, www.positive.news

---

How could you reduce the amount of negative news that you normally receive? What sources could you cut out or reduce – newspapers, radio, TV or Internet?

Try going for a whole week without access to any news and see how you feel. If there is something that you feel that you really need to know about you could always ask a well informed friend to give you a summary.

CHAPTER 10. HAVING DOWNTIME AND NOT MULTITASKING

"Multitaking? I can't even do one thing at once!"
– Helena Bonham Carter

I t has been found that one of the major causes of stress in our modern world comes from the ever increasing pressure to do, be and have more.

One of the most destructive unquestioned assumptions that we have in our society is that "more is better!" Our economies are based on an ever increasing Gross Domestic Product (apart from Bhutan who run their country using Gross National Happiness which you will learn about in Chapter 18). Businesses are constantly chasing higher profits and productivity, schools are moving towards data-driven striving for ever higher results and individuals are taught that they need to be, achieve and have more to be happy!

On the macro scale, it is crazy to be living on a planet with finite resources but be determined to constantly consume more and more. To sustain our present level of consumption we actually require the resources of 3 planet Earths! This is a way of living that we need to change rapidly if we are to leave a habitable world to our grandchildren.

Similarly, to constantly be demanding more and more of ourselves with our own limited physical, mental and emotional capacity is also unrealistic – it leads to increasing stress, illness, and unhappiness.

Taking time out to rest, relax, socialize and enjoy is really important. In today's busy world you may find that the best way to make this happen is to schedule it!

CREATE REWARDS AND POSITIVE ANTICIPATION

Making space to celebrate your achievements can make the process of work and life in general much more enjoyable. It can be all too easy to just keep doing things and completing tasks without taking the time to actually stop and really appreciate what you have accomplished. The practice of actually creating space to celebrate (and this may be as simple as doing a 30 second "happy dance") or to give yourself some form of reward, will not only create positive feelings in that moment but it will also make you more productive and your work or study process much more enjoyable.

Having things to look forward to in the future can also be a great way to raise your mood. This could be in the form of booking a holiday or scheduling a night out or a fun event. Then whenever you want a feeling of joy or excitement you can remind yourself of what you have planned.

This sense of positive anticipation actually stimulates the pleasure centers in our brains. A study by Lee Berk at Loma Linda University found that when participants were asked just to think about watching their favorite funny movie their endorphin levels (a happy hormone) increased by 27% and their human growth hormone levels by 84%!

These responses boost your immune system, reduce stress levels and create increased positivity in advance of, as well as at the time of, the actual experience. I would suggest scheduling your favorite movies straight away.

MULTITASKING – NOT SUCH A GREAT SKILL AFTER ALL!

Numerous experiments have shown that despite the popular belief that multitasking allows us to get more done, it is actually far less productive to work in that way. In our "always on the phone and checking emails" culture, this means that although people seem busier they are often less productive and creative. Every time that we are interrupted in our work, it can take 15 minutes to recover our focus and flow.

Bearing in mind that this state of flow is generally found when we are in the highly beneficial "engagement" level of happiness, it shows that multitasking interferes directly with our ability to be happy. It has also been found to raise our stress levels.

An experiment carried out at the University of London found that people who were multitasking had an average drop of 10 IQ points. To put this into context, this is the same amount that our IQ would drop if we went without sleep for 36 hours!

I don't know about you but I know that I really do not function well if I miss a night's sleep. Similarly, I have found that if I only have one task that I am focusing on and I remove any distractions from my environment then my creativity and productivity seem to explode.

DIGITAL ADDICTION

Most people do not see the constant use of mobile phones, notebooks, iPads and computers as potentially addictive but research and statistics point to a different conclusion. These technologies often are misused addictively and can result in many unexpected harmful problems.

A Time Mobility poll was recently used to assess people's relationship to their phones worldwide and discovered the following facts:

- 1 in 4 people check their phones every 30 minutes (1 in 5 check it every 10 minutes!)

- 84% said that they could not go a single day without using their phone.

- In the 25-30 year old age bracket, 75% said that they took their phones to bed (which, as you will learn in the bonus chapter about sleep, can have serious mental and physical health implications.)

The American Psychiatric Association have now recognized Internet Use Disorder (UID) as a serious mental condition that has many similarities to other addictive behaviors such as withdrawal symptoms, deception and obsession. Overuse of mobile phones and computers has also been found to cause stress, sleep disorders, limited attention capacity, eye strain, reduced social/emotional skill development and depression.

In China, Internet addiction has been designated as a national health crisis – 14% of China's youth are believed to be addicted! It has become a major concern of the Chinese Government who are actively attempting to reverse this problem.

Misuse of these technologies is also leading to more instant and dire impacts on people's lives. The American National Safety Council has reported that presently, 1 in every 4 car accidents is caused by texting whilst driving – that is about 1.6 million crashes every year in the USA!

An Exercise for the Digitally Addicted!

One way that you can reduce the constant ongoing stress and anxiety around being constantly "on call" is to have times in your day or week where you cannot use or be contacted by email or phone. If even the idea of this is scary right now then you might have to wean yourself off of it slowly. Start by "going off the cyber radar" for a couple of hours the last thing at night and then increase the time period as you are ready. You might be very surprised at the relief and relaxation that doing this can engender.

CHAPTER 11. JUMPSTART YOUR JOY

"Knowledge is of no value unless you put it into practice."
– Anton Chekov

Even though we have never met, I actually care about you! This may seem like a rather bizarre statement to make but it is surprisingly true. I care about you because I see you as part of my human family and I know that only when we all actively do our best to support each other in this family to become happier, kinder and more conscious will humanity go on to survive and thrive on this planet.

I wrote this book to inspire and enable people like you to become happier right now. I did not write this book just to be an interesting read or an expression of academic expertise. This book was written to facilitate your positive transformation.

For you to actually experience this shift you will need to take action and practice some of the exercises in this book. To make this much easier I have created two very simple, short routines that anyone can integrate into their lives. They have the potential to assist you to completely transform your experience of life.

TAKE THE CHALLENGE

I challenge you to do the *jumpstart to joy (J-2-J)* routine for 30 days and see what a difference it can make. Then, at the end of that period, if you love the changes you are experiencing you can carry on doing it. At that point, continuing may seem effortless because by 30 days it will have become a habit.

THE POWER OF HABITS

Most of our behaviors and ways of thinking have been created by default. We pick them up from our families and the culture that we are born into and then further develop them out of reaction, convenience, comfort or self-preservation. These ways of being are constantly being recommitted to by the many daily habits that we have.

An interesting study, by Duke University in the USA, looked at how much of our daily activity was carried out on a conscious basis compared to an automatic one. The conclusion was that over 40% of what people do on a daily basis is habitual. I would guess that an even higher percentage of our thoughts are automatic and repetitive! In the words of Confucius *"All men are the same, except for their habits."*

What makes some people naturally happier than others? They consistently practice certain happiness habits – either consciously or unconsciously.

So the key to enabling you to become happier is to find a way that you can easily adopt such habits – which just so happens to be what this chapter is all about.

If you are assuming that it can take a while and a lot of effort to create a new habit, you may be surprised and relieved to learn that it only takes 30 days and it can be relatively easy, if done properly, to adopt and integrate such a habit. The J-2-J has been designed in such a way that it is powerful yet undemanding, simple and even fun.

HABIT STACKING AND OTHER TRICKS

One of the challenges of making conscious choices and electing to do new things is that we all have a finite amount of willpower and we have to use that same limited resource for every type of decision that we make. This is called "ego depletion" and it has been extensively researched and studied. It means that we have a greater capacity to practice new activities and ways of thinking early in the day (or after naps). For this reason, the first routine to jumpstart your joy will be the first thing that you do in the morning.

To make it easier for you to practice the J-2-J you will benefit from something called habit stacking. Instead of having a list of separate new habits to try and do at some point in the day, we are going to connect a few simple habits together to do at one time, as one habit. In this way, it will require far less willpower because you only have to choose to do the routine and not each separate action. This need to use part of your limited daily willpower quota is further reduced by having already decided to do these daily routines at the beginning of your 30-day challenge and also by setting your intention just before you go to sleep the night before.

One of the barriers that can so often stop us from taking up a new habit is the concern that it will take too much time or effort. For this reason, I have deliberately kept these routines short and simple, whilst still maintaining their efficacy. You will find it easy to adopt these new routines because you are only making micro-commitments, so there is no need to feel overwhelmed.

You will also be using the concept of "streaking" to maintain your momentum by keeping track of your daily progress. Streaking refers to a process where we get a sense of achievement from creating a visual chain of successes. I have created a J-2-J 30 day tracking chart which you will find in your happiness toolkit. Every time that you complete either the morning or evening ritual you can tick it off on the chart. On a subconscious level, the longer your row of ticks, the greater your motivation to maintain and continue it becomes.

I am going to refer to these two routines as rituals from this point on. Both words refer to a set of actions that we repeat in pretty much the same way but routine can have an inherent sense of boredom or monotony, whereas, ritual brings a sense of magic with the expectation for some form of transformation.

"Motivation is what gets you started. Habit is what keeps you going" – Jim Ryun

BEFORE YOU BEGIN KNOW YOUR "WHY"

It is imperative that before you begin you are really clear about why you are ready to make these changes.

Take 20 minutes to sit down and answer these questions:

- Why haven't I chosen to be happier in my life previously?

- What will my life be like if I do not make this change?

- What positive changes would I like to experience in my life as a result of adopting these habits? How will my life look different? How will it feel different?

(You will find a guided visualization in the happiness toolkit that guides you through a clarification process in much greater depth than these questions can. It will be very helpful to go through the visualization at least once and definitely before you begin your 30-day challenge.)

Assuming that these questions have brought you to a place of clarity and enthusiasm for taking the 30-day challenge, then you are ready to move forwards. I suggest that you do five things:

- Print out and sign the "Happier Pledge" in your happiness toolkit. Put it up somewhere prominent in your home where you will often see it.

- Print out the Jumpstart to Joy 30-day tracking sheet. This will be very valuable for keeping your momentum rolling and for having an ongoing sense of achievement.

- Choose a start date to begin your 30-day challenge. The best date to choose is tomorrow!

- Decide upon a reward that you will give yourself on successfully completing the challenge. Obviously, you will be feeling more content, happy, positive, and inspired after doing a whole month of these practices but it can be great to actively celebrate and reward yourself for your efforts too.

- Go to the private online choosing happier page (request to join it, if you have not done so already) and declare your intent to the group or your joy buddies, that you are about to do the 30-day challenge. You can also post updates as you achieve each 10-day section of the challenge. At the same time, do comment on other group members' posts to acknowledge and applaud them for their commitments, efforts, and achievements. We are all stronger when we mutually support and celebrate each other.

HOW HAPPY ARE YOU NOW?

It can also be good to have a sense of where you are before you start on this journey. On a scale of 1 to 10 with one being totally unhappy and ten being ecstatic, where would you place yourself on average for the past few weeks? Make a note of this in your journal somewhere that you can look up again in a month's time.

PREPARING FOR YOUR RITUALS

Being prepared actually begins the night beforehand. Making sure that you go to bed at a good time and doing your evening ritual will set you up for a great sleep and a state of mind that will be conducive to a positive start in the morning. The morning ritual itself is an awesome way to become fully awake and energized for the day ahead.

Setting up a space where you can meditate, write in your journal and do some exercise will also make this process effortless. Remember, the fewer decisions that you have to make in the morning, the less will power you will require to carry out your morning ritual and other routines. You can choose your place of practice, type of meditation and exercise, music, clothes, etc., the night beforehand and have them set up and ready for your inspired start to the day.

Because you will be doing an evening and a morning ritual you will actually be in a "which came first – the chicken or the egg?" scenario.

Your evening ritual will set you up for and support your morning ritual and vice versa. Both practices are mutually supportive.

21 Minutes To Transformation

The minimum amount of time that you need to allot for these rituals to be effective is just 21 minutes – 16 minutes in the morning and 5 minutes at night. It may not seem long but because you will be using the optimal times for influencing your subconscious mind you will gain an amazing amount of leverage. Instead of your conscious mind attempting to affect your ways of thinking and being throughout your day, your subconscious mind (which is immensely more powerful) will start to have a positive influence on you.

Your Morning Ritual

This is what you will do as soon as you wake up every morning. You may have to wake up 20 minutes earlier each day to make this happen. In the scheme of things, this is not that much earlier but the positive impact it will have on your emotional state of well-being and your energy levels is well worth it. Getting up 20 minutes earlier in the morning can also be made easier by going to bed 20 minutes earlier at night. In Chapter 5 and in the bonus chapter about sleep, you will find some very useful information about how to optimize your sleeping patterns that will make this transition to earlier mornings easier.

It is generally best to get out of bed to accomplish your morning ritual. This will help you to make a faster transition into your waking life. Some people even like to have a quick cold shower first to really facilitate a speedy change-over. Having your morning ritual space set up previously, the night before, is really helpful. It is useful to have your clothes, cushions, journal, character strengths reminder card and perhaps exercise equipment and something to play music on already waiting for you.

The timings that I am suggesting are the minimum that you should aim for. If you wish to do any section or the whole ritual for a longer period, then please do, as it will have more of an impact. In particular, extending the length of time that you meditate or exercise for can be really helpful. However, doing this basic 16-minute ritual will be enough to have a powerful impact on your emotional well-being and your happiness set point.

THE FOUR GEMS OF JOY:

1. Meditation (5 minutes)

Use this time for any form of mindfulness, meditation, prayer or just to sit in silence.

This may be the most important thing that you do in your day. It is a chance to consciously connect with your inner self, to find a sense of inner calm and know that this is your essence – a valuable knowing to have later throughout your day.

In your happiness toolkit, you will find a pre-recorded smiling meditation which is a great way to start the day because it connects you up to your body's happiness circuit and stimulates your body to start releasing dopamine, serotonin, and endorphins. I recommend that you start with this.

2. Gratitude (3 minutes)

Write at least three things that you are grateful for in your journal. These could be about anything but make sure that they are different things each day. If you are not sure what sort of things you could be grateful for then you may like to consider the following topics: things, people, past relationships, health, work, play, opportunities, and experiences. It can be helpful to remember big things in your life but also think of simple, nearby things like your bed, last night's dinner, etc.

You do not have to write in great detail but it is worth contemplating why you are grateful for these things afterward and then to take a minute to drop your awareness inside to become aware of how these appreciations have made you feel.

Complete this part by asking yourself "I wonder what I will get to appreciate today?"

3. Acknowledging your Strengths (3 minutes)

Write a list of at least five of your natural qualities and skills before you start your 30-day challenge. These should include the character strengths that you discovered through doing the VIA questionnaire that you had a link to in Chapter 4. They may also include other positive virtues and talents that you are aware that you have or that others have told you that you have.

Every morning read this list out one by one beginning with the words "I am…" For example, you might say: "I am kind. I am grateful. I am curious. I am generous, etc." This is a chance to really acknowledge your merits. Pay attention to how you feel as you recognize and accept each aspect of yourself.

To complete this exercise, ponder the question of how one of your virtues might present itself on that day. For example "I wonder how I might express my kindness today?"

4. Exercise (5 minutes)

This is not necessarily your whole exercise routine for the day, although you could extend it and use it as such. Rather it is about priming your state for the day and waking up. Five minutes of exercise will release happy hormones into your bloodstream, invigorate your body and stimulate your thinking and creative capacity.

Do your favorite exercises, go for a brisk walk or even have a dance (maybe your happy dance?) – do whatever you will enjoy. It can be fabulous to exercise to the accompaniment of music, so potentially, this is a great time to put your happy playlist on and have fun.

If you would like to do specific exercises to strengthen or stretch your body but don't know what to do in such a short time period, you might like to check out some of the great apps for 5/7/10 minute workouts or short yoga routines.

OPTIONAL

Make your bed as soon as you get up. This may seem like a strange add-on but it can have a big impact. I heard the author Tim Ferriss talk about this. He said it was his most important morning habit because if life seemed overwhelming or chaotic it enabled him to get a sense of having some control and thereby massively reduced his stress levels. It generally takes less than 2 minutes, so why not try it?

Journal your dreams. If you are working with your dream wisdom, then you may need to write your dreams down first before going through your morning ritual.

Mirror Smiling or the Celebration Posture (3 minutes)

You could also add smiling at yourself in the mirror or standing in the celebration posture that you learned about in Chapter 8 (Using Your Physiology).

Extend the length of these practices

As stated at the beginning, 16 minutes is the minimum amount of time that is required to have an impact on your mental and emotional well-being. However, if you extend the amount of time that you dedicate to these practices, they will certainly have a greater impact on you. This is particularly true for your meditation/mindfulness practice and exercise routine. Taking more time to reflect on the things that you are grateful for and your character strengths can be beneficial too but keep your ritual enjoyable and only lengthen the time that it lasts to a time that and can easily fit into your morning routine.

***

YOUR EVENING RITUAL

This is best done when you are already in bed unless you are sharing your appreciations with other people in your life, in which case, you might want to do the magic moments section earlier and then contemplate them again, once you have retired to bed.

Magic Moments Appreciation (4 minutes)

Think back to three things that happened today that you can appreciate – moments, occurrences, experiences, opportunities, connections, etc. Write them down in your journal. If other people were involved then take a moment to consider and appreciate them too. Alternatively, as mentioned, you might like to share these appreciations out loud with friends or family earlier in the evening.

Set Your Intention (1 minute)

Just before going to sleep state this intention or something similar to yourself: "I am about to have a deeply nourishing and rejuvenating sleep. When I wake up at … (state the time that you have decided to awaken), I will feel totally refreshed, energized and ready for the day ahead of me."

OPTIONAL

Inspirational Reading (5+ minutes)

This may or may not fit into your schedule at this point in the evening but if it does, then this can be good to do before or after the Magic Moments. If you have other times in the day that are more conducive or easier for you to spend reading then choose those times. Reading can, however, be a very good way to wind down at night and prepare yourself for sleep. It is best to read real books at this time rather than a tablet or computer because the light can stimulate you back to wakefulness and disturb your sleep patterns. If you are using an e-reader, then have the settings on low light.

Reading inspirational books can have a valuable positive impact on the way that you perceive your world and provide you with great ideas and understandings that can enthuse your thinking. Books can be a great way to learn and having a sense that you are learning new things is a good way to increase your happiness. Alternatively, you may just wish to spend your reading time lost in fiction or fantasy novels for the sheer pleasure of the experience.

(Some great book suggestions can be found in the resources at the end of this book.)

***

CHALLENGES ON THE PATH

Resistance to early mornings – you may find the idea of getting up earlier to be daunting but remember it is only 20 minutes earlier and I am encouraging you to go to bed 20 minutes earlier too. If you follow the good sleep tips then you will have slept better anyway and the morning ritual is a fabulous way to become fully awake and energized.

The morning time is particularly valuable for doing this practice because your willpower reserve will be at its greatest, having not been depleted by any other decision making. So doing a series of stacked habits at this time can become effortless. Starting in this way can have so many positive knock on effects throughout the rest of the day, that you will probably soon realize that you much prefer to have a conscious and focused beginning every morning.

Not believing that you have the capacity for change or being happier – such a belief is probably based on your past experience. To that, I have one thing to say – **your past does not equal your future!** Do not allow such a limiting and false belief to get in the way of you discovering your greater potential. What would have happened if as a baby you had reached the grand age of 12 months and then decided that there was no point in continuing to try and stand up and walk like the big people around you because judging by your past experiences, you just were not cut out to be a vertically standing biped? Of course, that would have been crazy, but learning throughout life can be just like that. It can be hard, frustrating and seem impossible but if you keep trying and have an effective learning strategy then you will generally be able to learn any new skill or way of being.

Concern that other things may get in the way – be prepared. Sit down and write a quick list of all of the things that you can imagine getting in the way of your practice. Then write a list of brilliant things that you could do in response to those challenges. Now if any of them do actually happen, you are prepared and can automatically respond in an effective and helpful way that will allow you to still practice your rituals.

Missing a session – don't worry, it happens. Sure your tracking sheet won't look perfect but that is OK. Just re-commit to your 30-day challenge and carry on doing the best that you can. Certainly, do not mentally berate yourself about it – that really will not bring you happiness!

It can also be an opportunity to learn what things can block you in life and get in the way of your commitments. Look for patterns and triggers, then consider how you can avoid them or respond to them more effectively in the future.

Having to deal with cynics and naysayers – there will always be people who have pessimistic or self-limiting beliefs that they wish to push on to those around them. The best policy is to ignore their words but be compassionate towards them – after all, it can be a painful way to experience life from that perspective.

Feeling alone and/or unsupported – it can certainly be tough if you are living in an environment which does not support you in making positive changes. Having people on your side who will encourage you to step into living your full potential and be happier is profoundly valuable. This is exactly why I set up the private online community. There you can support and celebrate each other by posting your commitments and achievements as well as commenting on other members' posts to encourage and applaud them. You can also post a request for a joy buddy who you can team up with to have greater direct support.

ASSESSING YOUR 30 DAYS

Once you have completed your first 30 days take the time to assess what impact it has had and how you feel within yourself.

On a scale of 1 to 10 with one being totally unhappy and ten being ecstatic, where would you place yourself on average for the past couple of days? Check what score you gave this a month ago.

How have your levels of contentment, happiness or even joy been throughout the 30 days? How has your creativity or productivity been? How have your relationships been? How resilient have you felt in times of crisis or challenge? What changes have you experienced?

It can also be good to ask "how could I make it better?" Could you add more happiness habits, do the rituals for longer, find friends to do the J-2-J with, etc.?

If this month has been good for you, then you could just carry on doing these rituals as they are now part of your lifestyle or you could commit to another 30 days (or 60 or 90!)

FLEXIBILITY AND ADAPTION

The J-2-J rituals consist of some of the most effective and potent practices to raise your happiness levels on a consistent basis. I would encourage you to do all of them because their compound effect is so much more when they are done together. However, you may need to adjust the rituals in some way so that they work better for you, create some variety or so that you can enhance them further.

To deepen the practices, probably the best thing to do would be to lengthen your morning ritual. Longer meditation and exercise would both be useful but keep them to a time that is still feasible for you. You may need to get up earlier to do this but that is fine because by this point you will know that you can adjust and improve your sleep patterns around your new morning routine, as well as be enthused by the many benefits that have come from having such a fantastic habit.

Variety is important because it keeps us interested and often makes things more enjoyable. In the context of the J-2-J, you may find that doing different meditations, exercises and adding new qualities to your list of strengths will provide you with helpful diversity. The very nature of the gratitude and magic moment exercises requires that you constantly find things, experiences and people to appreciate, so these are already versatile as they are.

To enhance the J-2-J rituals further, you may wish to add on other self-empowering habits such as visualizations, affirmations, breathing techniques, spiritual practices, smiling in the mirror, or any of the other exercises that have been previously presented in this book. Now that you have this basic foundation it can be much easier to adopt new habits. Just do not try to do too much, as you always want to keep these rituals easy to do and enjoyable.

CONGRATULATIONS

I hope that you have been inspired by this chapter and can already sense the potential that these rituals offer. However, it is not enough to just know about that potential because if you do not actually try them and experience the results then all that you have done is collect more intellectual knowledge which may be interesting but not necessarily useful or correct. When we actually experience things and know them to be true then we have taken the profound step of moving from having knowledge to having wisdom.

I encourage you to dare to commit to doing these rituals from tomorrow onwards. Do not wait until you have finished the book before you start them. You can keep reading this book at the same time as you begin to experience and embody the wisdom of these pages.

Creating simple, new happiness habits is the key to empowering you to be able to make permanent, affirmative changes in your life. By consciously choosing to adopt such habits, you are taking the reins and creating your life how you actually want it to be.

You are about to go on an amazing inner voyage of self-discovery and personal growth by embracing this 30-day challenge and practicing the jumpstart to joy rituals. I would like to acknowledge you for being keen to learn how you can grow and live in a better way because there are many people out there who have never considered the possibility that life could be anything other than how it has always seemed to be. It takes a certain courage and an open mind to embrace this learning path. So salutations to you on your journey – you are awesome!

***

To support you with your morning and evening rituals you will need the *happiness toolkit* which you can download for free. In it, you will find a happiness pledge, a 30-day ritual tracking chart, the J-2-J reminder card, a strengths and qualities card, plus a guided intention visualization and a smile meditation MP3 digital recording. You can download these at Reader Bonus Materials

The *My Happiness Journal* could also be very helpful for you to maintain these rituals on a daily basis. You will be sent information about how you can buy it at a discounted price when you download your happiness toolkit.

Being connected to others who are also adopting the jumpstart to joy rituals will make this transition much easier too. This could be friends and family who would like to accompany you and make positive changes in their lives or it could also be by joining the online Choosing Happier community. Here you can gain mutual support, encouragement, and connection. You can also put out a request for people to become your *joy buddies* (specific people who will encourage you on your journey to joy and vice versa – this personal level of accountability and support can be invaluable). If you announce when you are starting your 30-day challenge, your progress as you go through it and its completion, it will allow others to champion you and celebrate your achievements and transformations with you.

Go to http://www.choosing-happier.com/community and ask to become a member.

I am excited about the shifts that you will experience in your life and the positive impacts that you will have in the world around you too. If you would like to share your experiences, do please post them in the online community. I love to read or hear about the impact that the J-2-J has on people.

PART 3

THE WAYS OF BEING

PERSPECTIVES AND ATTITUDES FOR HAPPIER LIVING

The previous chapter's exercises are all designed to have a major impact on your ability to be happy. You will find them to be most helpful when you try them out and practice them regularly. This next section offers fewer exercises for you to try but it does provide some really important understanding about the attitudes and habits that will support you to expand your happiness. If you can grasp and practice these approaches to life thereby altering your behavior, then you will find that your capacity to be happy will grow tremendously.

CHAPTER 12. GUIDANCE BY JOY

"Follow your bliss." – Joseph Campbell

This recommendation by Joseph Campbell could be one of the sagest pieces of advice that you ever hear.

If we are open to the possibility that our natural state of being is one of happiness, then it would make sense that whenever we become more aligned with this natural state then we will start to feel happier. As such we can use those feelings as an internal guidance system that can put us back on a path of balance and connection that is aligned with our true selves.

Sadly, most of us get conditioned to follow our "should" rather than our bliss. These are the externally based directives that we believe that we have to do to be acceptable in the eyes of our society, our religion, our family and our friends.

These "shoulds" may sometimes be for our highest good but often they are more about maintaining societal control or stability and as such may not be for our highest good or that of those around us at all. Many horrendous acts and wars have previously occurred in our human history because people did not stop to question whether following the shoulds and the instructions that were dictated to them were right or not.

In the 1960s, some literally "shocking" experiments were carried out at Yale University to understand how and why people were able to carry out atrocities during WW2. In the Milgram experiment, volunteers were each told to give increasingly high electric shocks to another volunteer (who they could not see but could only hear) whenever that person got the answer to a question wrong. The invisible volunteer was actually an actor who would shout, then scream and then finally beg not to be shocked, as the fake voltage meter continually increased to what would have been fatal levels. Disconcertingly, most of the volunteers actually overrode their consciences because they fell into a conditioned pattern where they felt compelled to obey the commands of the authority figure.

If they had really been administering those levels of electricity to the other volunteer it would have resulted in serious injury or potential fatality. Yet 65% of the volunteers did so because they were told to do so and because they believed that as such they would not be held personally responsible! This to me is the peril of training people to obediently and unquestioningly do whatever they are told.

Yet incredibly we all have an inner moral compass that can tell us what is right and true for us do. It might take a change of behavior to remember to do it and a bit of practice to clearly recognize it and then act on it, but it is actually very easy to use. All we have to do is to feel inside ourselves whenever we are considering options. If an idea or action brings us a feeling of happiness, joy or bliss (and this is an open-hearted feeling) then it is likely to be our path and our best option. If on the other hand, we discover an uncomfortable or "icky" feeling then it is probably not the direction or action that we should be taking.

The film "The Bucket List" with Jack Nicholson and Morgan Freeman is a fabulous example of a couple of guys reconnecting with and doing the things that bring them joy. Sadly their motivation for doing so was that they were both facing terminal illnesses. I highly recommend that you do not wait until that point!

Much of your happiness and success in life will come from your courage and capacity to follow your joy. To this end, I highly recommend that you practice pursuing the options in your life that give you this sense of joy.

Following your bliss in the moment can give you clarity on what would be the better option in the present but it can also be valuable in helping you to become aligned with your true life direction and way of being. This is, in fact, a helpful way of finding your purpose and the value of living with an awareness of your purpose is exactly what we will look into that in the next chapter...

CHOOSING WITH JOY

You can begin to practice following your bliss whenever you notice that you have a decision to make. Start with simple decisions and build up to bigger ones. Consider each option and notice what feelings it engenders in you. Follow the choice that feels good inside and drop any option that feels icky.

N.B. It can take practice and discernment to do this in situations where some form of fear may be part of the picture too. Sometimes following a certain path may initially seem an uncomfortable option because of that fear. If you do feel fear then I recommend that you find a way to shift it with movement (dance, jog, cycle, etc.) because this is a powerful way to process, transform, understand and let go of emotions. Afterward, check back in to see how you feel.

Chapter 13. Having Purpose

"True happiness… is not attained through self-gratification, but through fidelity to a worthy purpose." – Helen Keller

Do you have a sense of where you are going in your life and why? An incredibly valuable way to increase your positivity, your energy levels, and your resilience is by having a clear purpose that guides your life. When we are clear and inspired by our purpose and a higher vision we are constantly supported in our actions by this driving force which gives us motivation, inspiration and an enjoyment of the sense of alignment that we feel in our lives.

On another level, when we have a commitment to our purpose it seems to enable the potential of unexpected support from the "Universe" to flow into our lives to help us. This is beautifully summed up in this passage by the Scottish mountaineer W. H. Murray:

"Until one is committed, there is hesitancy, the chance to draw back, always ineffectiveness. Concerning all acts of initiative (and creation), there is one elementary truth, the ignorance of which kills countless ideas and splendid plans: that the moment one definitely commits oneself, then Providence moves too. All sorts of things occur to help one that would never otherwise have occurred. A whole stream of events issues from the decision, raising in one's favor all manner of unforeseen incidents and meetings and material assistance, which no man could have dreamt would have come his way."

Murray said that he had been inspired by this passage from Goethe's "Faust":

"Whatever you can do or dream you can, begin it. Boldness has genius, power and magic in it." – Goethe

LIVING A MEANINGFUL LIFE

When this purpose is a form of positive contribution on this planet and is therefore for the greater good, it becomes a doorway to living a meaningful life. The meaningful life was the 3rd type of happiness that was defined by Martin Seligman. This is the most sustainable and deep form of happiness. It is characterized by knowing what your main character strengths are and using them in the service of something larger than yourself. It is when we find a way to serve the greater good that we find profound meaning and purpose and as a result, great happiness.

HOW TO CONNECT WITH YOUR PURPOSE

"Efforts and courage are not enough without purpose and direction." –
John F Kennedy

This may be your big purpose in life, the reason that you are here or it may be your present purpose in life. We are not all lucky enough to have one clear and obvious major life purpose. For many, it may be an evolving and changing series of purposes as we move through life. If that is the case for you then the trick is to keep tuning into your inner guidance and your joy to constantly be aligned with what your present purpose is.

AN EXERCISE TO HELP YOU BECOME CLEARER ABOUT YOUR PURPOSE

If you want to get clearer about what your purpose actually is then here are some questions that can help you to find more clarity. Take 20 minutes to answer these questions, writing whatever thoughts arise as quickly as you can so that there is more opportunity for this flow to uncover some gems of understanding.

- What is important to you?

- What truly inspires and uplifts you?

- What do you really want (and not just to have)?

- What are your values?

- What do you stand for?

- What do you want to be remembered for?

- What local or global issues attract your attention?

- What would you do if you knew that you could not fail?

- When do you feel most energized and alive?

- When do you feel really happy, joyful or at peace?

"Learn to get in touch with the silence within yourself and know that everything in life has purpose. There are no mistakes, no coincidences, all events are blessings given to us to learn from."
– Elisabeth Kubler-Ross

CLARIFYING YOUR BIGGER PURPOSE

Ask yourself what sort of a world you would really like to live in. Ponder your answer and imagine some of the most magnificent aspects of this amazing potential world. Then ask yourself:

"What can I do to make this better world a reality?"

"What talents, skills, passions and resources do I already have that I could use to help this reality to manifest?"

GAINING MORE CLARITY AND FOCUS IN YOUR DAY

It can also be very helpful on the day to day level to actually connect with the purpose behind every action that you take. By asking yourself "What is my outcome?" whenever you are engaged in any activity it will enable you to stay focused and much more effective in all that you do. This is *living your life with purpose* and it will also support you in living in a happier state.

THE DALAI LAMA'S THOUGHTS ON PURPOSE

I apologize for quoting one person so many times throughout this book but I do love this man's clarity, peacefulness, humor, humility, generosity, joyfulness and compassion. I also value the many gems of wisdom that he shares and in this particular case, I would like to reference another very poignant one. The Dalai Lama has said that the very "Purpose of Life" is the goal of avoiding suffering and discovering happiness.

CHAPTER 14. SELF-COMPASSION

"Remember, you have been criticizing yourself for years and it hasn't worked. Try approving of yourself and see what happens."
– Louise L. Hay

Another invaluable tool for not getting caught up in our negative emotions and self-judgment is the practice of self-compassion. This is about learning to be emotionally responsive to our own suffering from a place of kindness.

How do you treat yourself when things go wrong? So often our inner dialogues can be very judgmental, critical and harsh. In fact, if a friend or loved one were in the same difficult place that we find ourselves in we would not dream of speaking to them in the same way or tone as we often experience in our own self-dialogue.

We are subject to many internal voices that interweave in our consciousness to form our personality and our perspective of reality. One of these voices is the inner critic which is often very quick to berate and put us down for any mistake that we make. The *inner critic* voice is created by the unfortunate amount of negative feedback that many children receive whilst growing up and also because the brain is wired to naturally remember more negative comments than positive ones. We end up believing that this voice has a valid view of life and rarely question its accuracy. However, that is exactly what we need to do.

Ask yourself these questions now as a means of exploring self-acceptance:

- "Who am I without my stories from the past?"

- "When I look at myself without the filters of self-judgment, what do I see?"

> *"Self-esteem isn't everything it's cracked up to be because a lot of people who have high self-esteem feel so good about themselves that they feel entitled to abuse and use other people! The question then is how can you get people to feel good about themselves without just elevating their sense of superiority and the answer to that question seems to lie in the concept of self-compassion."*
> – Professor Mark Leary

I need to qualify that self-compassion is not the same as developing high self-esteem which has been a prevalent pursuit and practice in our modern world. Although having high self-esteem can be useful in some ways, it is not inherently a benevolent state of consciousness. There are many people with high self-esteem who end up using and abusing others or the environment because it can encourage the feeling of superiority.

Whereas self-esteem involves thinking about how good you feel about yourself and how positively you evaluate yourself, self-compassion involves how you treat yourself when things go wrong. As we develop the ability to be self-compassionate we naturally become more kind with others as well. We move from a place of seeing ourselves in isolation to a place of recognizing our common humanity and the challenges that we all share.

"Success is total self-acceptance." – Viktor Frankl

As a person who has learned to be self-compassionate, you will find that you accept yourself, are less afraid of failing, less of a perfectionist, less self-critical, less anxious and more content and effective in all that you do, at peace with yourself and of course… happier.

TIPS FOR DEVELOPING SELF-COMPASSION

Firstly, it is important to give yourself permission to make mistakes and have hard times because this is the reality of the human experience. Mistakes are an inevitable and essential part of the learning process. Many highly successful people are where they are today because they were willing to make more mistakes than other people in the search for their answers and their successes.

Hard times and difficult experiences happen to all of us – it is just the nature of life. So remember that you are not alone and that there are over 7 billion other people on Earth that have faced and are facing really difficult situations too.

"While you can't control your experiences, you can control your explanations."
– Martin Seligman

Secondly, practice becoming aware of your inner critic's voice and not over-identifying with it.

When you catch that voice berating yourself, ponder whether you would actually say such things to a close friend who was having a hard time. Now simply say in your own mind "Thank you for sharing but I am choosing to be kind to myself instead in this moment."

Then take a long deep breath with full awareness before asking yourself what you might say to someone else in the same situation. Either reflect on the answers that come to you or actually write them down.

At the same time, as you are becoming mindful of your inner critic and giving it less validity, you are also learning to develop and create a strong inner relationship with your self-compassionate voice.

The last thing that you can do when you recognize that your inner critic has been active is just to use your inbuilt mammalian response to touch and give yourself a hug or rest your hands on your heart. You might be quite surprised to discover how such simple actions can instantly impact your thoughts and feelings.

CHAPTER 15. PRACTICE OPTIMISM

"A pessimist sees the difficulty in every opportunity, an optimist sees the opportunity in every difficulty." – Winston Churchill

An element that has been found to have a big influence on people's happiness and well-being is how they perceive their reality. It turns out that wearing rose-tinted glasses actually is a helpful way to see your world because optimists are happier, more effective and generally more successful in many areas of life.

An optimist will assume that good things are permanent and everywhere in their lives whilst also see bad things as temporary and limited to that particular time and experience. Such bad things are often perceived as a chance to learn and grow. Holding this perspective enables them to unconsciously always be on the lookout for opportunities and good things to enjoy and take advantage of.

By comparison, a pessimist will assume that bad things and experiences are permanent and everywhere whilst good experiences are a matter of luck and are therefore rare and unlikely. This means that they often miss out on good experiences because they do not recognize them or make the most of them as they happen. Worse than that, it means that they are always unconsciously scanning their world to find evidence to affirm their negative beliefs about reality – which can result in them experiencing life as limited, difficult and hostile.

It is important to be clear that being optimistic does not require that your life situation is great or advantageous. The example of Viktor Frankl who ended up in a Nazi concentration camp illustrates this fact very clearly. Things could not have been more dire for him and yet he and some of the other prisoners were able to maintain their optimistic viewpoint by focusing on having a higher purpose or being in loving service to their fellow camp mates. As a result, they were able to survive their atrocious situation in a better state of mind.

Being optimistic can put you in a positive upward spiral of life experiences whilst conversely being pessimistic can put you in a downward spiral of life experiences.

From a light-hearted perspective, the advice from Monty Python in the song "Always Look on the Bright Side of Life," is actually quite good, even if it is perhaps a bit oversimplified.

"Always look on the bright side of life
If life seems jolly rotten,
There's something you've forgotten
And that's to laugh and smile and dance and sing."

PESSIMISM CAN BE BAD FOR YOUR HEALTH!

An interesting study has recently been carried out by University College London. They monitored 163,363 people who had been diagnosed with various forms of cancer over 14 years and discovered that those who were most distressed and anxious about their cancer were up to 4 times more likely to die from the disease! Conversely, those who had an optimistic outlook were more likely to recover or live longer.

ASSISTED BY YOUR UNCONSCIOUS

This process of always being on the lookout for positive opportunities is facilitated by an aspect of the brain called the reticular activating system (RAS). This is a collection of neuronal circuits connecting the brainstem with the cortex. Its role is partly to scan our surroundings for clues and signs that increase our potential for survival. In its evolutionary context, it meant that our subconscious mind would perpetually be watching out for signs of food sources or potential dangers so that we could instantly respond to the opportunity or threat.

The RAS also acts as a filter system that only allows the most significant information through to our conscious mind – rather like a biological spam filter. It has been estimated that our brains receive 200 million bits of information per second from our environment. This is a colossal amount of data and far more than our brains are able to process and understand. In fact, our brains are only able to process about 134 bits of information per second! Without our RAS we would become quite overwhelmed by the sheer quantity of information that our senses are capable of receiving.

You may not have known what was occurring at the time but you have no doubt previously experienced your RAS in action. Perhaps this happened when you had just bought a new item such as a phone or a car. Having researched the market and found or bought your new, ideal phone or car you may have been surprised by how often you suddenly started to see it everywhere! Your unconscious mind had registered that that phone/car was very important to you and therefore, began recognizing it and letting you know that there were more of them whenever they came into your area of perception.

Your RAS is also the part of your brain that allows you to notice some-one saying your name in a crowded room despite the high noise level.

If you are presently wired for pessimism your RAS can be incredibly unhelpful because it will only see dangers and a negative reality. This will raise your stress levels whilst reducing your levels of creativity, productivity, success and of course happiness.

By comparison, the RAS of an optimist is a very supportive mechanism because it is searching for positive experiences and opportunities which invoke the pleasurable feelings of happiness and gratitude. These will, in turn, lead to more optimism because the more that we see positive opportunities and events the more we will expect that trend to continue and to be our reality.

THANKFULLY YOU CAN CHOOSE TO BE OPTIMISTIC

If people were either optimistic or pessimistic because of their genes or unalterable early conditioning then it would be quite distressing to discover that you were a pessimist for life. However, it has been clear-ly shown that optimism can be learned through practice. (Martin Seligman has written a book on the subject called "Learned Optimism" that I highly recommend you read if you would like to dive more deeply into the subject.)

So it is good news to know that we are able to train our brains to scan our worlds for the ideas and opportunities that will allow our success rates and our happiness to flourish.

"It's more than a little comforting to know that people can become happier, that pessimists can become optimists, and that stressed and negative brains can be trained to see more possibility." – Shawn Achor

---

Consciously developing the practices of gratitude and appreciation as outlined in part one of this book is most definitely the foundation for making this shift to greater optimism. Apart from writing down what you are grateful for in the morning and writing down what you have appreciated each day in the evening, you could also try this exercise occasionally.

THE DEEP DIVING POSITIVE EXPERIENCE REFLECTION EXERCISE

Whenever you have had a particularly amazing or great experience, set aside 15 minutes to reflect upon and write down everything about it. In particular, ask yourself and discover what you really appreciated about it, why you appreciated it, who helped make it happen, what aspects of yourself enabled it to happen and most importantly how it makes you feel when you remember it.

(For this last question about feelings, it is best to tune into the bodily sensations that are engendered by remembering the experience rather than needing to find the correct descriptive words.)

If you find yourself particularly prone to pessimistic thoughts then you might find the following suggestions really helpful...

TRANSFORMING PESSIMISM

You can develop your optimistic mindset by becoming more conscious of when you have negative thoughts and then choosing to think differently.

Recognition of pessimistic thoughts can happen because you have chosen to be more aware of, and are investigating, the negative responses and beliefs that you have. You may also become aware of these thoughts by being attentive to your energy. Often when we become pessimistic or negative our energy levels drop or there are some obviously uncomfortable feelings that we experience. The more that you can recognize these thoughts or responses when they happen, the more possibility there is to choose optimism.

Once you have noticed the pessimistic thought pattern you can use the following ways to turn these thoughts around to a more optimistic perspective.

Reframe it. Look for the upside of the situation by asking yourself questions like **"What can I learn from this?" "What good thing could happen now that this situation has arisen?"** or **"If I was the type of person who could overcome this challenge and thrive in this situation, what would I do?"** (Should you come up with a creative answer to this last question, then do it!)

Challenge the thought. Simply respond to the negative thought by saying to the pessimistic part of your mind "Thanks for sharing but I am going to respond differently this time."

Distract yourself. Sometimes it can be useful to just change your focus to something more enjoyable for a while. Dancing, exercise, movement, and listening to uplifting music can be very helpful.

Step back for objectivity. You may find it useful just to write down the negative thoughts that have come up. This will help you to see them from a more neutral perspective.

Change your physiology. Whenever we drop into a negative place we adopt certain ways of standing, sitting, moving and even breathing that reflects this feeling as well as helping us to maintain it. For example, a depressed person may slouch and collapse their posture, look downwards with guarded eyes and breathe shallowly. By contrast, when we are feeling positive and optimistic we tend to stand straighter, lift our chests, look forwards with bright engaging eyes and breathe deeper. So try changing your physiology to that of an optimist and see what happens!

Dispute the pessimistic thought. Just because you have a thought it does not mean that it is true! Nor is a thought a fixed aspect of you – thoughts and beliefs often change through time. What we hold as real and true today can easily become false and untrue tomorrow, so be open to questioning whether your thoughts or beliefs are really accurate.

TRANSFORMING PESSIMISM QUESTIONS

- "Is it true?"

- "Can I be 100% certain that it is true?"

- "What evidence is there that it is true?"

- "Have I blown it out of proportion?"

- "Are there alternative explanations?"

- "What is the effect of thinking this way?"

- "If I cannot prove that it is true what other ways could I think about it?"

You will often find that you cannot be 100% certain that a pessimistic perspective is true, in which case you are free to use a new, more empowering or positive thought or belief instead. If you cannot prove that either of these viewpoints is 100% correct then why not choose the one that will be most likely to lead you to a happier and more fulfilling outcome.

(You might want to write these approaches and questions down and put them somewhere obvious to remind yourself or carry them with you to use them in emergencies! There is a pre-printed version that you can download now with your free Happiness Toolkit that is part of the Reader Bonuses.)

Be aware that each thought that you have will either move you towards happiness or away from it, so it is important to pause and evaluate the direction of your thoughts as often as you are able to.

MEDITATIVE OBJECTIVITY

Learning to develop a greater awareness of pessimistic thoughts and beliefs that influence us is greatly supported by having a meditation practice. Regular meditation will allow you to develop a certain space between yourself and a thought, thus enabling you to see it more objectively rather than believing that it is true and just the way that it is.

I highly recommend that you find a way to explore and integrate meditation into your life – even if it's only for 12 minutes a day! (See the meditation chapter for ideas and suggestions.)

BLESSING THE NEGATIVE

Another helpful tool to use that can help us to remain positive in the face of negative or difficult situations/people is the power of blessing. By blessing I mean *to recognize and bring forth the good in any situation, person or condition.* Whenever we focus on the negative, we give it power, so this practice neutralizes that tendency and helps us to find the positive opportunities more quickly or at the very least, not to carry the weight of that negativity in our own hearts.

THE BLESSING PRACTICE

Whenever you are faced with a negative situation or person in your life, do the following:

1) Take a deep breath and quieten your mind.

2) Stop complaining or talking negatively to anyone else about it.

3) Bless the situation or person in your own mind.

The practice of blessing can, of course, be applied to positive situations and people too. It is yet another way to practice and express gratitude in our daily lives.

CAN YOU BE OVER-OPTIMISTIC?

The very nature of the word "over" explicitly implies that you can be. Therefore, of course, you can be over-optimistic (or over-anything) and this type of optimism is called *irrational optimism*.

To be so optimistic that you expect only positive outcomes would be sure to lead to problems because life continually throws us unexpected curve balls and disappointments. However, the optimistic perspective that I am recommending is a more balanced, reasonable and realistic optimism where difficulties and problems are seen as part of life too. What is more, they are embraced as challenges and learning opportunities with the intention of overcoming them and thereby building one's character and resilience from the experience of doing so.

As we learn to be more resilient and to maintain an optimistic viewpoint when faced with setbacks we will experience less stress, be better at coping and also be more open to recognizing any helpful opportunities that may arise during the process. In essence, we will be more effective, successful and happy.

CHAPTER 16. BEING HUMAN

– Embracing All Of Our Emotions

"You cannot protect yourself from sadness without protecting yourself from happiness." — Jonathan Safran Foer

As mentioned at the start of this book, the goal is not to eradicate or avoid all of our "negative" emotions. Our emotions are part of the whole experience of being human. However, it is important to learn how to express them appropriately (in a way that harms no one including yourself), to be able to release them and to not get stuck in them. At the same time, it is important to strengthen our experience of positive emotions which will make us less susceptible to the negative.

UNCONDITIONAL ACCEPTANCE

To be really free and open to regularly experiencing joy in our lives it is necessary to embrace all of our emotions and express them appropriately. There are no wrong emotions, although how we act in response to certain emotions may be unhelpful or harmful and therefore unwise. Emotions are just our "energy in motion." Naturally, some emotions feel better than others and actually this can be used as our inner guidance system to encourage us to go towards the behaviors and thoughts that create good feelings.

One of the problems with attempting to suppress negative emotions is that they actually end up feeling stronger and having an impact on us and our well-being for longer (for some people that can be their whole lives!)

As a result, these emotions often end up controlling us and distorting our view of the world because we have put so much energy into suppressing and denying them. A wiser choice is to accept our difficult feelings instead and then choose a productive and kind response to those feelings. In effect, we give ourselves permission to be human.

PAIN IS INEVITABLE, SUFFERING IS OPTIONAL

There will always be painful or difficult situations in our lives. That is the nature of being a human on planet Earth. Pain is when your life conditions do not match your expectations and your model of the world. Suffering is when your life conditions do not match your model of the world and you feel powerless to do anything about it.

Suffering is optional. We can always do something to change the experience of pain, even if it is on the level of small changes. Pain can be lessened by our remembering that it is just another part of life's rich tapestry of experiences and by getting support to be with it or move through it. In this way, we remind ourselves that we are not powerless.

EMOTIONS ARE TRIGGERED BY THOUGHTS

Most emotions that we experience arise in response to particular thoughts that we have had. Sometimes this happens so fast that we are not even aware that we had a thought before the emotion overtook us!

It is valuable to realize that just because we have had a thought does not mean that it is true, helpful, valid or necessary to obey and conform to. So as well as giving ourselves space to experience and express our emotions appropriately, it is also important to attempt to become conscious of the thoughts that have triggered these responses.

If you discover any thought patterns that are really not serving you, then use the suggested techniques in the previous chapter to challenge and change them.

THE PAIN-BODY

Eckhart Tolle uses the term "pain-body" to describe a semi-autonomous accumulation of old negative emotions in our energy field which we all have to a greater or lesser degree. He asserts that pain-bodies feed themselves by latching ones focus on negative situations and dramas that resonate at a similarly harmful frequency. Once triggered, a pain-body will hijack one's whole thinking process. Not only that but it also replenishes itself by stimulating negative responses in others and thus awakening their pain-bodies. In this way, both pain-bodies can mutually energize each other because they crave both inflicting and suffering pain. To the pain-body, pain is pleasure.

This description of the negative patterns that we can get caught in can be very helpful in enabling us to separate ourselves from our automatic behaviors and to realize that we are not the emotions that sometimes course through us when we are triggered. As such, it can give us a greater freedom not to react when there is negativity around us.

The more that we avoid such reactions and learn to stay in the present, the more that we are able to think clearly and choose to respond in ways that are truly aligned with our wiser selves.

> *"The pain-body is an addiction to unhappiness."*
> – Eckhart Tolle

From a brain function perspective, it is also possible to understand the triggering of the pain-body as being the shift to the amygdala which looks for negative patterns in our environments and to the brain stem that triggers the fight, flight or freeze responses. Unfortunately, these parts of the brain are unable to see or allow for consequences and therefore make poor decisions and often respond very destructively. Therefore, the goal is to keep using or at least return as soon as possible, to using the prefrontal cortex part of our brain which is much better at assessing situations and making wise decisions.

FORGIVENESS

Some of the emotions that we particularly struggle with are anger, hatred, resentment and bitterness. These often arise because we have had the experience of being wronged by someone or a belief that a past situation was unfair. However, we hold on to the emotional distress that surrounded that particular event long after it has past. Often memories of it will inhibit us from interacting with certain people or in particular situations that remind us of the original painful experiences, even when they are actually quite different. Being attached to the trauma of past experiences can have far-reaching consequences in many areas of our present day lives. One of the most effective ways to dissipate these types of negative emotions is to use the powerful tool of forgiveness.

Forgiveness does not mean that we need to believe that something that was done was actually ok or that we are willing to have it happen again. Rather we are letting go of the idea that there is a debt that someone has to pay. When we stay resentful we hold on to our anger so that the person who perpetrated the act and everyone else knows they were wrong or because we believe that doing so will protect us from similar situations happening again. Worse still, some of us actually end up directing the anger inwardly with the mistaken belief that we were somehow to be blamed for it happening. For some people, it may manifest as a constant background fear that something bad could happen again and this overwhelms them and inhibits them from moving forwards in life. Sometimes it is things that we have said or done ourselves that we struggle to forgive.

"Resentment is like taking poison in the hope that someone else will die."
– Anon.

We can find ourselves bound to this anger, hatred or fear, hoping that it will protect us from further pain. Sadly this strategy will, in fact, cause more pain and harm in the long run. Often our continuing pain will also impact other areas of our lives and those around us. A malicious act that was done to us many years ago, if it was not done thoughtlessly, perhaps was meant to hurt us once by that perpetrator in that moment. However, we end up ceaselessly replaying the incident in our minds, repeatedly stirring up the feelings of pain and distress. In some ways, our own minds can end up being far more unkind to us than the original person who wronged us was ever able to be. On top of this, holding resentment towards someone often does not impact them at all!

Forgiveness is a self-healing process that leads to greater freedom and happiness. We are choosing to stop the cycle of negativity and pain and we are primarily doing this for ourselves. It is a process of empowerment whereby we take back our own power and stop giving it away to people from our past. By choosing to forgive we are releasing ourselves from future pain and the negative consequences that have impacted our lives due to having held that hurt.

Interestingly, the power of forgiveness can have a massive impact on our physical as well as our mental and emotional health. There have been over 1200 studies since 1997 that have looked at the impact of forgiveness on our well-being. In a research project by the Luther College in Iowa, they concluded that there is a very strong correlation between having a lot of stress and poor mental and physical health for the majority of the population except in people who were highly forgiving of themselves and others. Fred Luskin Ph.D. from Stanford University has been studying the impact of forgiveness and in *Forgive for Good* describes not forgiving or holding a grudge as "caustic" and says that "it raises your blood pressure, depletes your immune system, makes you more depressed and causes enormous physical stress to the whole body." Living in "unforgiveness" has also been shown to be associated with an increased risk of heart disease, stroke, and cancer.

Forgiveness is often a process and may require revisiting several times as you go through layers of that pain and resentment. Just know that it gets easier the more that you practice it. There are many different ways to actively work with forgiveness but first, you need to make the decision that you are willing to do so and then be willing to try the forgiveness processes that you discover when you look for them.

I have several techniques that I use when I work with coaching clients around forgiveness issues and it certainly can be helpful to have an experienced coach or therapist for support, especially if you have held unforgiven wrongs for a long time. To this end, you may want to research local or online coaches or therapists who work in this field to facilitate your process. Sometimes just having a committed intent to forgive and some simple exercises to do on your own can be really powerful too. The "Heart Meditation" CD (and book) that can be found in the Resources section at the end of this book can also be a very valuable way to regularly heal levels of past anguish as well as to create more joy in your being.

> "Forgiveness is the only way to heal ourselves and to be free from the past. Until we can forgive the person who harmed us, that person will hold the keys to our happiness."
> – Archbishop Desmond Tutu

Another way that we can learn not to get stressed or caught in our negative emotions is by developing our resilience skills…

Chapter 17. Developing Resilience

"The greatest glory in living lies not in never falling but in rising every time that we fall." – Nelson Mandela

Our resilience is our ability to withstand, deal with or recover from setbacks, adversities, and challenges. It is also our ability to cope with and handle stress. Developing new resilience skills is an indispensable way to improve your experience of life and to be happier.

We all have different resilience capacities, some of which are based on our level of health (and the level of anti-stress nutrients in our bodies,) our level of regular exercise (which help us cope better with stress) and whether we have good relaxation and self-nurturance habits. However, much of our capacity also relates to our mental and emotional conditioning around dealing with adversity.

Study after study has shown that if we are able to conceive of a failure as an opportunity for growth, we are more likely to experience that growth.

We all face stresses and challenges in our lives and this is not necessarily a bad thing. There are actually healthy and positive levels of stress. Facing adversity and finding ways to overcome it often results in our self-growth. Yet sometimes we can get stuck and overwhelmed instead. The good thing is that we can easily learn new skills that enable us to improve our resilience.

"Things do not necessarily happen for the best, but some people are able to make the best out of the things that happen." – Tal Ben-Shahar

---

The University of Pennsylvania created the Penn Resilience Program. They taught a program of resilience skills to school children who were in very challenging situations and prone to depression. The results were quite astounding as they reduced the incidence of depression by 50% in these kids (as compared to a control group of children in the same situation.) This was a figure attained by assessing them two years after they had gone through the training – these were skills that literally transformed their lives from then on.

Resilience skills have since been taught in schools and colleges, as well as in high-stress occupations such as the medical profession and the military because they have been found to be so effective.

"Only those who dare to fail greatly can ever achieve greatly." – Robert F. Kennedy

---

The essence of resilience training is the understanding that problems, adversities, and failures are part of life's journey and are actually essential for us to grow and succeed. In fact, the more willing we are to fail, the higher our chances of succeeding become. Knowing this can be enough to allow us to reframe a situation from being a "nightmare disaster" to just being the next learning opportunity and exciting challenge!

To support you with changing your perspective and response to difficult situations, you will find the questions that I mentioned in the chapter on optimism to be very helpful.

"What can I learn from this?"

"What good thing could happen now that this situation has arisen?"

"If I was the type of person who could overcome this challenge and thrive in this situation, what would I do?"

An interesting aspect of our minds is that they have a tendency to dramatize and imagine worst-case scenarios happening as future possibilities. So one resilience skill is being aware that our fears are likely to be ungrounded fantasies, which enables us to pause and consider other possible outcomes.

It is also valuable to recognize that the human race has evolved through adversity and we are surprisingly able to adapt and respond to even extreme situations. If the worst-case scenario actually becomes a reality we are likely to discover that our *fear* of this consequence is actually much worse than the actual experience of it.

> *"It's not the adversity itself but what we do*
> *with it that determines our fate."*
> – Shawn Achor

The ability of individuals to experience positive growth in the face of extremely challenging or traumatic circumstances has been termed adversarial growth or post-traumatic growth. These positive shifts made in the face of great loss, pain, illness or from being in extreme situations have been well documented and can be very inspiring. Learning about them can also be part of the process that can enable you to reframe the concepts of disaster and failure. There are lots of great books or videos about people who have had powerful adversarial growth experiences and I highly recommend that you occasionally read or watch them for inspiration. (Some suggestions can be found at the end of this book.)

Many techniques and understandings that are used in resilience training are also positive psychology approaches and have already been covered in this book. Part of resilience training is about learning and understanding what strengths, strategies, insights and resources you already have to deal with challenging situations. In this way, you can build on them and use them when you actually need them, as well as develop new ones that will also help you.

"There is only one way to happiness and that is to cease worrying about things which are beyond the power of our will." – Epictetus

The topic of resilience and the diverse skill sets that are taught around it are worthy of another book that just focuses on these. There are several that I recommend if you are interested to know more and I have included them in the Recommended Books section. There are also some useful courses that you may wish to research and explore. I have included a link in the Resources And Tools appendix to the College of Wellbeing which has a very accessible and practical course, as well as the original courses by Penn University.

PART 4

EXPANDING HAPPINESS

CHAPTER 18. THE BUTTERFLY EFFECT

– Impacting Your World

*"You have been created in order that you might make a difference.
You have within you the power to change the world."*
– Andy Andrews

The "Butterfly Effect" is the concept that small causes can have large effects. It was originally used as an expression by Edward Lorenz, a mathematician and meteorologist, to account for the unexplainable anomalies which were found in weather models. The idea was that the flapping of a butterfly's wings could potentially have an impact on the formation and direction of a hurricane in another part of the world several weeks later.

In a similar way, the impact of one person's actions, words, facial expressions, emotional energy and behavior can have unexpected far reaching effects on many other people. With the Internet, this can occur at great distances almost instantly, in a way that was inconceivable even two decades ago!

Hopefully, you have already begun practicing some of the exercises in this book (or will do so very soon) in which case you may already be experiencing greater levels of happiness, joy, creativity, productivity, contentedness, connection, etc. However, you may also have noticed that the world and the people around you may seem to have become happier as well. This is the result of two factors: firstly a change in your personal perspective allows you to interpret and perceive the elements that make up your world in a more positive way; secondly, that your greater happiness will have a direct positive effect on those around you that inspires them towards a happier state of being as well.

IMPACTING YOUR WORLD BY THREE DEGREES

Recent research about the impact of modern social networks and the Internet has shown that we are deeply affected by more people than we ever were before. In the book *Connected,* the authors James Fowler and Nicholas Christakis conclude that it can be shown that we have the potential to directly impact people within three degrees of ourselves, for example, my niece's boyfriend's mother! In their research they discovered that if a friend's friend's friend put on weight, it could significantly increase the likelihood that you too would put on weight. In the context of this book they also discovered that if a friend's friend's friend became happy, you also were more likely to become happy! I therefore suggest that you choose your friend's friend's friends carefully!

The average 3-degree reach is about 1000 people but for some people who are very social, well-connected or perhaps because their work requires them to directly interact with lots of people (e.g. teachers), the influence of their way of being could be far greater.

The one person that you can have the biggest impact on in this world is yourself and this book is all about giving you the tools and mindsets to enable you to live in a happier way. This should be your goal. However, it is heart-warming and exciting to know that your journey to greater happiness will also have an indirect, positive effect on many other people. If you become happier, so potentially will your friend's friend's friends.

The potency of such an amazing level of connectivity is summarized by James Fowler and Nicholas Christakis when they note that: *"If we are connected to everyone else by six degrees and we can influence them up to three degrees, then one way to think about ourselves is that each of us can reach about halfway to everyone else on the planet."*

THE IMPACT OF OUR BEING AND OUR DOING

So how we are can have an unforeseeable effect on the world around us that is quite empowering, rewarding and exciting to realize, especially when we are actively choosing to be more positive and happy. Yet there are also direct impacts that are experienced by those around us when we act in compassionate and caring ways. This brings us back to the practice of random acts of kindness and similarly compassionate behaviors.

A quote from the Dalai Lama that I used earlier highlights the value of compassion in the world very clearly: *"If you want others to be happy, practice compassion. If you want to be happy, practice compassion."* Fascinatingly, it is not just the person who receives an act of kindness nor the person who acts altruistically who receive the benefits of such caring behavior...

ELEVATION

When a compassionate or kind action takes place anyone who witnesses this act will be positively impacted. This ripple effect is called "elevation."

This is the experience of uplifting positive thoughts and feelings that any observer of an act of kindness has. In two experiments carried out by Simone Schall at Cambridge University, they discovered that people witnessing acts of kindness (which they termed "prosocial behavior") would experience positive emotions and also would then be more inclined to be helpful, kind and altruistic themselves. The ripples move outwards...

MORE BUTTERFLY WING BEATS

Taking this concept further, if someone who witnesses an act of kindness is more likely to act kindly to another person, then this is another powerful, positive incident that can potentially impact a further range of people within three degrees! The ever increasing expansion of concentric circles of positivity that move outwards definitely inspires hope.

"Be the change that you wish to see in the world." – Mahatma Gandhi

MIRRORING

The discovery of what have been called mirror neurons is part of the explanation for why we end up copying the positive actions of others, whether that be smiling or acting compassionately.

Have you ever noticed yourself unconsciously smiling at someone instantly when that person smiles at you? It may even have caught you unawares. This happens because of mirror neurons which are designed to help us learn skills, languages, and behaviors as well as to support rapport and connection on a social level. They enable us to imitate the expressions or actions of another person within milliseconds.

Fascinatingly, they often enable us to feel that other person's emotional response too. This is due to them triggering the release of the associated neurochemicals or molecules of emotion that are released in the body in response to changed physiology and visualized experiences.

Once you are well practiced with the habits of happiness that I have laid out in this book you will also probably notice and enjoy how much the mirror neurons in the people that you come into contact with are unconsciously triggered, leading them to smile and be happier as a reflection of your state.

A HISTORICAL PERSPECTIVE

You may not have considered it before but the expansion of compassion-based organizations is a relatively new and ever-increasing phenomenon. When I say compassion-based organizations I mean ones that were set up by people to support and protect the interests of other people or the environment that they were not necessarily or directly a part of themselves. Until the 19th century, there were very few organizations around the world that had been created purely for the benefit of others rather than having been formed out of some self-serving motivation. Most groups were set up to support, protect and strengthen their own rights and power. Yet in the last 150 years, the growth of associations and groups purely created for the benefit of others has expanded at an unprecedented rate.

One hundred and fifty years ago there were probably less than ten truly altruistically based groups and now it has been estimated that there are possibly about half a million with more being created every week.

These new altruistic groups form an essentially unconnected, non-ideologically based, egalitarian movement that wants to make this world a better place for everything and everyone. They are generally based on the belief that there should be care, equality and justice for all people as well as care and protection for our environment.

There are probably even more unaccounted for groups which may be very small but are nonetheless heart-warming and will have some kind of effect. A fabulous example of one of these was recently provided by my friend's daughter, Jess, who was excited to announce that she and her friends had set up a new environmental concern group at her school in Australia. It is very unlikely that teenagers would ever have conceived of such an idea 100 years ago, let alone actually acted upon it and set something up. What is more, in today's cyber-connected world such groups can potentially have quite an impact. How many more tens of thousands of such groups might there be around the world?

You may be asking yourself why I appear to have gone off on an interesting but slightly obscure tangent. Well, it is precisely because I believe that the growth of these care based organizations is a fantastic example of elevation. The more that we see that other people are actively caring for distant and unrelated members of their human family and for the animals and ecosystems of this planet, the more we actually experience that kindness within our own physiology and are in-spired to act altruistically ourselves.

CHAPTER 19. CONSCIOUS HAPPINESS AT A NATIONAL SCALE

"If you have the power to make someone happy, do it. The world needs more of that." – Anon.

It is incredibly exciting to know that we can actually change our own levels of happiness and as a result also improve our health, creativity, productivity and potential to be successful in so many areas of our lives. It is even more exciting to know that by doing so we are having a positive impact on many people around us which is likely to bring about more acts of kindness and the benefits of increased happiness for those people too.

HAPPIER INSTITUTIONS

Choosing to live more happily is not just an individual practice. There is great value for institutions to adopt these principles because they will become more effective in all that they are doing too. This is already beginning to be explored in schools, colleges, and businesses.

Schools that have begun to adopt the principles of positive psychology and resilience skill training have seen remarkable improvements in children's grades, creativity, and disposition. Even more importantly, they have given their students invaluable skills that enable them to cope with life's challenges and to thrive once they have left school.

Similarly, many businesses are investing in training for their staff to learn and adopt many of the valuable understandings of positive psychology which results in greater productivity, creativity and success for these companies. The book *The Happiness Advantage* written by Shawn Achor focuses on the value of happiness in the business world which is where he does most of his consulting work. I love the idea of there being "Happiness Consultants" (although perhaps Shawn uses a more formal job description for his work).

But how far can this scale up? How big an impact can happier living have? Can actively working towards a happier way of living go far beyond the individual, the group or the company? Could it expand to a fundamental way of being and viewing the world on a national or international level? As it happens such an approach is already being practiced...

BHUTAN

Bhutan, the ancient Buddhist Kingdom in the Himalayas, is about 15,000 square miles (39,000 square kilometers) and rises to 23,000 feet (7,000 meters) above sea level. It is surrounded by China along its northern borders and India along its southern borders. There are only about 770,000 people in Bhutan but they are possibly some of the luckiest people on the planet.

GROSS NATIONAL HAPPINESS

Bhutan is a totally inspiring example of what can be done when we hold happiness as an essential part of life at a national level. In 1972 the King of Bhutan adopted the philosophy of Gross National Happiness as a foundation for the running and development of the country. Gross National Happiness (GNH) was seen as a valuable, practical, sensible, conscious and sane alternative to the internationally used Gross Domestic Product (GDP) which is traditionally used to measure the "success" of most countries.

GDP is purely a monetary measure of the final value of all goods and services that are produced annually or quarterly by a country. As such, it encourages ever-increasing consumption no matter what the cost to the people or to the environment and is, therefore, a destructive and very short-term way of perceiving how well a country is doing.

By contrast, GNH focuses on measuring the factors that are linked to well-being in a country's population and to its long-term sustainability. Bhutan's core principle is "development with values." It would seem to be a much wiser way of measuring how successfully and sensibly a country is developing.

There are 4 pillars to the Bhutanese model of GNH:

1. Sustainable development
2. Preservation and promotion of cultural values
3. Conservation of the natural environment
4. Good governance

All decisions made by the government have to take GNH into account. How different would our countries in the West be if this was the principle that our laws and legislations were based on instead of often being created in favor of corporations whose most important goal is profit whatever the cost?

This approach has also meant that Bhutan actually has a negative carbon footprint because care for the environment and long-term sustainability are so essential to the government and local decision-making processes.

In the Bhutanese Constitution it states: *"The Government shall ensure that to conserve the country's natural resources and to prevent degradation of the ecosystem a minimum of 60% of Bhutan's total land shall be maintained under forest cover for all time." (The Constitution of the Kingdom of Bhutan, article 5, section 3.)* Presently it is covered by 72% forest. They have also made massive investments in clean hydro-electric projects that already provide energy for neighboring parts of India as well as for themselves.

Knowing about the Bhutanese approach to life might not seem to be of much help to you when you are living elsewhere in the world but it might just make you smile inside and become more open to the possibility and value of whole communities, companies or even countries giving precedence to happiness. If GNH can work so effectively for one country then it is certainly a principle that could be adopted by other countries.

HAPPIER COUNTRIES

Whilst I was traveling around the world I found it quite fascinating how much happiness varied from country to country. These differences were mostly a reflection of the varied perspectives and values held by the various cultures (and maybe sometimes were a reflection of the climate because sunnier climates can lead to sunnier dispositions).

Sometimes, the variations can be traceable to differences that arise because of an individual concept that is fundamental to the way that a particular culture interacts. Two great examples of such cultural-centric concepts, can be provided by Thailand and Scandinavia.

In Thailand, there is a word and concept known as *Sanuk*, which loosely translates as to have fun. In fact, it is much more than this because it can more accurately be translated as "striving to achieve satisfaction and pleasure from whatever you are doing." Within the inherent playfulness of sanuk, there is also a deep sense of caring and social connection.

I have lived and worked in Thailand and experienced first-hand how deeply integrated this concept is in every aspect of life there. Finding ways to have sanuk in almost everything that the Thais participate in is essential. I even noticed that if there was work to be done that did not have a sense of sanuk to it, it was often seen to be better not to do it at all! As a contrast to growing up in the UK with what is termed the "protestant work ethic," I found this attitude to be very refreshing. Thai people themselves are quite lovely to be around and it is not by accident that Thailand is known as *the land of a thousand smiles.*

There is a concept in Scandinavia that means "just the right amount." In Swedish the word is *Lagom*, in Norwegian it is *Passe* and in Icelandic it is *Mátulega*. This concept deeply permeates these societies' ways of looking at the world. It infers that "it is always best to have just enough" which is in stark contrast to the excessive "more is better" approach of modern consumerism.

No doubt, it is because the value of just enough is so deeply ingrained in the Scandinavian psych, that the Icelandic public took such a strong stand when they faced such a massive financial economic crash in 2008. The crash was caused by the reckless actions of some of their bankers, but unlike elsewhere in the West where the bankers and financial institutions who caused the devastating turn of events were let off, in Iceland the bankers who had been making these bad decisions were actually held responsible and sent to prison! The Icelandic government also took the unprecedented actions of allowing the banks to fail and bailed out the poor debtors rather than the wealthy banks. As a result of their unorthodox response, the Icelandic economy is thriving once more. By contrast, other Western economies who faced similar financial crises but dealt with them by penalizing the poor with austerity measures whilst bailing out the banking institutions who had actually caused the crashes, are still struggling. This radically different response symbolizes the value of knowing that just enough is great, rather than what can be seen as a greed based concept of more is always better.

The concept of *lagom* also infers that "we can be enough just as we are" which is the antithesis of the core wound of "not being enough" that is so often found at the root of many Western psychological imbalances. Growing up in a world without a sense of inherent lack is bound to lead to a greater sense of happiness and contentment with life and oneself. No doubt this is partly why the Scandinavian countries tend to score very highly in the comparison tables of national happiness.

MEASURING WORLD HAPPINESS

Over the last decade, there has been an increasing interest in measuring national happiness as a way of determining and comparing the real health of various countries. It is obviously challenging to be able to accurately gauge what the levels of happiness may be for any particular country and it will always be a generalization, however, there have been some interesting reports and charts made that attempt to quantify and compare happiness levels around the globe.

THE WORLD HAPPINESS REPORT

In 2012, the United Nation's Sustainable Development Systems Network commissioned *The World Happiness Report.* They recognized that happiness was a more important and proper measure of social progress and in essence, the real goal of public policy. The report scores nations on responses to the life evaluation questions collected in the Gallup World Poll and includes variables such as real GDP per person, healthy life expectancy, corruption levels and social freedoms.

The report found the top 10 happiest countries to be: Switzerland, Iceland, Denmark, Norway, Canada, Finland, Netherlands, Sweden, New Zealand, and Australia. The USA came in 15th (one place below Mexico) and the UK came in 21st (one place behind the United Arab Emirates). When comparing the whole list, the average score of the top 10 is more than twice as high as the bottom 10.

Social factors and strength of networks were found to be one of the most important influences on happiness levels, as was illustrated by an interesting observation that was made about the impact of economic recession on happiness. The economies of Iceland and Ireland were decimated during the financial crisis, however, their happiness scores remained high because their citizens have very strong social connections.

In alignment with the whole philosophy of this book, that it is possible to learn how to be happier, the report also offers a study from neuroscientists who found strong evidence that you can increase your happiness in the following ways: practicing mindfulness training or meditation, taking a less commercial approach to life, and giving or volunteering.

THE GROSS DOMESTIC PRODUCT FLAW

"The gross national product measures everything except that which makes life worthwhile." – Robert Kennedy

There is, however, a serious flaw with the UN's World Happiness Report and that is that they use an individual GDP figure as part of the calculation. As I stated when talking about Bhutan, this does not take into account the harmful impact of increasing consumption, the loss of natural resources or damage to the environment. These things will have a major impact on people's ability to be happy and healthy especially in the long-term. Crucially, the pursuit of ever increasing production is irreconcilable with the reality of living on a planet with finite resources. Certainly, GDP growth on its own does not mean a better life for everyone in any given country. It does not reflect inequalities in material conditions between people or properly value the things that really matter to people like social relations or how they spend their free time.

In the face of this, it is helpful to have a broader and more conscious way of measuring how well countries are doing.

THE HAPPY PLANET INDEX

A much more sensible measurement is offered by the *Happy Planet Index* which was created by the New Economics Forum. This measures levels of health and happiness against sustainability by taking the well-being and longevity of a population, measuring how equally both are distributed and then setting the result against each country's ecological footprint. Using this way of ranking means that the most successful countries are those where people live long and happy lives at a minimal cost to the environment.

The results of assessing the countries of the world in this way are remarkably different. The nordic countries that normally do so well in the international happiness comparison lists are not found at the top. Instead, it is mostly Latin American and Asian Pacific countries.

Top of the list is Costa Rica, followed by Mexico, Colombia, Vanuatu, Vietnam, Panama, Nicaragua, Bangladesh, Thailand, and Ecuador.

Norway is the only Scandinavian country to be found in the top 20. The USA ranks 108th out of 140.

Costa Rica really stands out from the crowd in this index and is worth looking at in more detail. The average life expectancy is 79 ½ years (average life expectancy in the USA is 79 and in the UK it is 81). Its literacy rate is 97.8%. (By comparison, according to the US Department of Education 32 million US citizens or 14% of the US population cannot read!)

Costa Rica tops the Happy Planet Index because it maintains really high levels of health and happiness whilst only using a quarter of the resources that are typically used in the Western world for the same standard of living!

So why is Costa Rica such a happy, healthy and sustainable country? Well, mostly it comes down to having a history of forward thinking and inspired policy making. They abolished their army in 1949 and instead chose to invest in creating a robust health and education system. At present 99% of their energy comes from renewable resources and they are fully committed to being carbon neutral by 2021. As such, they are another shining example of what is achievable.

The Happy Planet Index provides a compass to guide nations, and shows that it is possible to live good lives without costing the Earth. When countries adopt this approach to measuring their success, then policy making is likely to change radically. The index encourages us to live in a more sustainable, fair, equitable, healthy and content way – that is definitely something worth pursuing and celebrating.

WORLD HAPPINESS DAY

"Happiness for the entire human family is one of the main goals of the United Nations."
– Ban Ki-moon, former UN Secretary General

I hope that you can see that some people and countries are already recognizing the value of developing happiness. You might also like to know that there is now an International Day of Happiness – March 20th which was created by the United Nations.

In 2011, the UN General Assembly adopted a resolution which recognized happiness as a *"fundamental human goal"* and called for *"a more inclusive, equitable and balanced approach to economic growth that promotes the happiness and well-being of all peoples."* Secretary General Ban Ki moon said, *"We need a new economic paradigm that recognizes the parity between the three pillars of sustainable development. Social, economic and environmental well-being are indivisible. Together they define gross global happiness."*

So the great news is that happiness is being taken seriously on national and international levels – which would seem to be a delightful oxymoron to end this chapter on.

In Conclusion

I hope that you have enjoyed this journey into the many facets of happiness. Even more than that, I hope that you have been inspired and actually begun to experience the benefits that arise from doing the various exercises that I have presented throughout the book.

In brief summary, I would like to remind you that being happier is:

> ➢ a skill
> ➢ a practice (built on simple habits)
> ➢ an enabler (it will improve other aspects of your life too)
> ➢ <u>and your choice!</u>

So go forth and enjoy the continuing journey. May it bring you much joy, balance, fun, and contentment. May the ripples of your cheerfulness, gratitude, care and kindness travel out far and wide to help create a wiser, more balanced and compassionate human presence on this beautiful planet Earth.

ONE MORE THING...

If you enjoyed this book or found it useful I'd be very grateful if you'd post a short review on the bookstore website from which you purchased it. This enables potential readers to get an idea about the book before buying it and encourages bookstores to promote it. Your support in this way really does make a difference and I read all the reviews personally so I can get your feedback and make my books and the tools that I provide even better.

Similarly, if you have enjoyed this book and got a lot from it then please pass it on, buy it for someone who might benefit from it or recommend it to friends, family and colleagues, and let people know about it on your favorite social media platform.

I believe that the information in this book could really help a lot of people and have a valuable impact in the world. The more people there are who find it easier to live in a more compassionate, kind, generous, resilient, happy, and joyful way, the better off we all are.

Thanks again for your support and I wish you a joyful and happier life from now on.

A SPECIAL INVITATION

(In case you missed it the first time.)

છે૪ઝ

G oing it alone and trying to make positive changes on your own can be very challenging. By comparison, having the support of being connected to other like-minded people who are attempting to make similar positive shifts can make such a transition much easier, more enjoyable and quite invaluable. To this end, I have created a Facebook community page that is for readers of this book who would like such support. This FB page is a place where everyone can share their gratitudes, successes, challenges, support, inspirations, "happy dances" or random acts of kindness. It is also a place where you can find "joy buddies" to help keep you accountable to your practices and commitments to living in a happier, kinder and more generous way.

I check in personally on the page and moderate the posts to keep them on track. When I have time, I even respond directly to posts and comments, so it will be great to connect with you there.

If you would like to be part of this community and gain that mutual support, encouragement, and connection in an ongoing way, then just go over to http://www.choosing-happier.com/community and ask to become a member.

છે૪ઝ

Bonus Chapter: How to Improve Your Sleep

There are many habits that you can adopt and tools that you can use that will greatly enhance the quality of your sleep. Below I outline the practices that will support you at various stages of day and night. I also provide an easy-to-follow list of some of the best tools that I have come across to support better sleep.

DURING THE DAY

It is important to spend time in natural sunlight outside or if you are limited to being in darkened spaces indoors, then it is best to be under blue/white lighting that mimics sunlight, inhibits melatonin release and stimulates the mind.

IN THE EVENING

It is important to reduce the amount of blue/white light in your environment so that your mind can begin to slow down and relax. This is best to do for 2-3 hours before you intend to go to sleep. Our bodies are designed to naturally begin producing melatonin, the sleep-inducing hormone, in response to the reduction of light in our environment and especially the absence of blue/white light.

Having a technology curfew where you commit to not using your computer, tablet or phone after a certain time in the evening is really helpful.

Light emitting e-readers, computers and phones used just before sleeping (or worse still, intermittently through the night), can have a very negative impact on your sleep. A study carried out by the Brigham and Women's Hospital, in Boston, found that reading e-readers before bedtime prolonged the time it takes to fall asleep, delayed the circadian clock, suppressed levels of the sleep-promoting hormone melatonin, reduced the amount and delayed the timing of

REM sleep, and decreased alertness the following morning! So avoid using any light emitting screens for at least an hour before going to bed.

The excessive brain and eye stimulation that occurs with late (and through-the-night) use of smartphones and computer games is having a massive negative impact on many people. It would be great if there were more information in the mainstream about this, as well as the harmful effect of sleeping close to the electromagnetic fields that phones emit, because most people are really unaware of the negative impact that these can have.

Having a *"night-time wind-down ritual"* an hour before going to sleep can be invaluable. This could include having a bath (with epsom salts or relaxing aromatherapy oils), fiction reading, gentle stretching, meditating, journaling and sharing your favorite parts of the day and other appreciations with your loved one(s).

TOOLS AND TECH TO IMPROVE YOUR SLEEP

There are several useful tools and habits that you can use to create optimal light conditions. I will describe them in detail here and you can find links directly to them on the Choosing Happier website http://www.choosing-happier.com/great-sleep-resources

F.lux is an app that can be added to PCs which changes the computer's light spectrum to be aligned with your actual local time zone. This means that it reduces the blue light and increases the yellow in your screen. In this way, the body still starts to produce melatonin at the appropriate time. This handy app is free and well worth using.

Wearing blue-blocking sunglasses or gaming glasses in the evenings can also have a similar effect.

Dimming your lights in the evening or using the Phillips Hue Smart Lights which can be set to dim and change to the yellow/white spectrum in the evenings whilst beginning the day as blue/white light, is another option.

AT NIGHT

It can be helpful to make your bedroom into a real *sleep sanctuary*. Have a great mattress, clean bed sheets, a good pillow and maybe use relaxing aromatherapy oils before sleeping. Keep the space free from TVs, computers, and work.

To enable your body to drop into a really deep sleep, it is important to sleep in a completely dark room with minimal light or sound interference. Using blackout curtains, blindfolds (especially the *mindfold* – a really brilliant blindfold that completely blocks any light, even in the middle of the day which means that it is perfect for midday naps too) and turning off or covering up all light emitting gadgets in your bedroom are useful ways to keep your room dark. If your nights are disturbed by noise, you could consider getting a white-noise machine to cover them up or using good quality ear plugs.

The perfect sleep temperature is apparently around 65 degrees Fahrenheit (18 degrees centigrade), so adjust your bedroom's temperature and the thickness of your duvet to be close to this temperature, if you can.

ROUTINES, EXERCISE AND SLEEP

Having consistent sleep routines is really important. The more regular that you are with the times that you go to sleep and wake up, the more easily your body will be able to drop into a natural, stable and dependable circadian rhythm.

It is best not to do any rigorous physical exercise for 2-3 hours before going to sleep, as this can make going to sleep less easy. By contrast, it is very useful to do some form of exercise shortly after waking or as Shawn Stevenson, the author of the book *Sleep Smarter* says, "A good night's sleep starts the moment that you wake up!"

If you are often beset by worries that keep you awake last thing at night, then I suggest that you do this exercise:

WORRY JOURNALING

Write a list of all of the things that you need to do and a list of all of the things that you are worried about. Now place the lists nearby and commit to letting go of all thoughts about them until the morning!

This may seem too simple but it is based on the principle that late at night is our least effective time to solve problems. By contrast, we are most creative and efficient in the morning, plus our subconscious minds are able to process information as we sleep. Therefore, contemplating our challenges and worries before sleep is extremely unproductive and unhelpful. Knowing this makes it easier to drop these thoughts every time that they arise because we become aware that we will be able to address them more successfully in the morning.

By contrast, you will find it much better and more productive to contemplate the things that you can appreciate and be grateful for in your life, as you drift off to sleep.

CLEAR POSITIVE INTENTION

Remarkably, how we expect our sleep experience to be can have a massive impact on the way that we feel when we wake up. Often our last thoughts before falling asleep are among the first thoughts that we have in the morning. So if you go to bed feeling concerned that you will not have enough time for a good night's sleep and will, therefore, feel lousy and tired during the day, then you are likely to manifest exactly that. Conversely, if you are just about to have a short night's sleep but are thinking about something exciting that you will be doing the next day, like going on holiday, then in all likelihood you will wake up feeling great.

For me, it was the experience of going on a couple of holidays where I only had 4 hours' sleep before I had to get up again to head to the airport for early flights, that really made me stop and question why my sleep experience was so different. Normally, 4 hours' sleep would have put me into a semi-zombie state the following day but somehow when it was the beginning of an exciting holiday that did not happen. I realized that both my thinking before going to sleep and my thoughts upon waking were the two factors that were different from my normal way of responding to short sleep times. Since then, I have consciously set a positive intention just before I drift off. It has allowed me to radically change my sleep patterns.

Knowing that your last thoughts can have such a powerful effect on the quality of your sleep and waking experience, it is wise to choose intentions that will facilitate better sleep such as "I am about to have a deeply nourishing and rejuvenating sleep. When I wake up at ... I will feel totally refreshed, energized and ready for the day ahead of me." Find words that work for you and try it to see how different your morning experience can be.

NUTRITION, DIET, HORMONES AND SLEEP

Poor sleep can also be associated with the lack of certain nutrients. Making sure that they are in your diet or in some cases, taking them as supplements, can be very helpful. The most relevant nutrients are generally magnesium, selenium, potassium, calcium, omega 3 oils and vitamins C, D3, and B6.

It has been estimated that about 80% of the population in the USA and the UK are deficient in magnesium. It is probably the most important deficiency for many people to address because magnesium has a vital role in calming the nervous system and relaxing muscle tension. One of the main symptoms of magnesium deficiency is chronic insomnia. Magnesium can be found in green leafy vegetables, nuts, seeds and seaweed. Having hot baths with epsom salts is also a great way to absorb more magnesium.

The hormone serotonin is well known for bringing about feelings of happiness, improving mood and cognitive abilities. It is also the building block for melatonin creation and is, therefore, crucial for regulating your body's internal clock. Melatonin's role is to encourage and enable us to go to sleep more easily in the late evening. The best way to make sure that your body is able to create adequate amounts of melatonin at the right time is to make sure that your body is able to produce good quantities of serotonin and to avoid the blue-white light spectrum in the evenings.

Most serotonin production happens in our intestines with the help of various strains of healthy bacteria that live there as part of our gut biome. Maintaining a healthy gut biome is, therefore, incredibly important if we want to be able to produce lots of serotonin. Taking good care of the gut biome is supported by eating fermented and probiotic-rich foods (kefir, sauerkraut, tempeh, miso, kimchi, live yogurt, etc.) whilst avoiding pesticides (found in non-organic foods), unnecessary antibiotics, excessive sugar, chlorinated water and diet soda drinks.

N.B. Melatonin is available as a supplement in many countries but the quantity within each tablet is far too high. Most supplements contain between 3-5mg. This is ten to fifteen times more than required as we only need 0.3mg. For this reason, it is best to avoid taking these high dose melatonin supplements on a regular basis, however, for the occasional support with jet lag these high dose supplements should be fine.

AVOID EATING JUST BEFORE SLEEPING

Our bodies can release incredibly beneficial growth hormones at 3 potential times in normal day to day living – when we fast, exercise or just after we go to sleep at night. These hormones are very important for keeping us really healthy and able to resist many degenerative diseases. Few people fast regularly (although I highly recommend learning how to do so and adopting this habit), and many people do not exercise enough which leaves the one remaining option for receiving a systemic burst of life enhancing growth hormones – going to sleep at night! However, the body will not release these hormones if it is in digestive mode. Practically speaking, this means that you need to avoid eating for 2 hours before you go to sleep for maximum benefit.

DREAM JOURNALING

For many people, dreams are just strange nonsensical imaginings that happen at night whilst others do not remember having dreamt at all. We actually all dream every night and our dreams are very important for our mental and emotional health as they enable our minds to process our daily experiences. Sometimes, our dreams can also teach us things about ourselves and are a profound source of inner wisdom.

The best way to develop a relationship with your dreaming mind and begin to understand the meaning and messages in our dreams is to keep a record of them upon waking up. This can be done in a beautiful journal or there are also phone apps where you can easily keep a record of them.

GREAT SLEEP RESOURCES

There is a page of useful links to all of the apps, tools, equipment and books that I have mentioned in this chapter, on the Choosing Happier website. Whenever I discover more useful tools, I will add them to that page. You can find it at:

http://www.choosing-happier.com/great-sleep-resources

APPENDIX 1. HAPPINESS TOOLS AND RE-SOURCES

A more extensive and very inspiring list of useful sites and tools that is being constantly updated can be found here:

http://www.choosing-happier.com/recommended

To become happier in your daily life the first thing that you need is a commitment to the simple practices and new ways of thinking outlined in this book, that can engender a happier and more positive state of mind.

THE CHARACTER STRENGTH SURVEY

To discover what your top character strengths are, take the online survey for free at www.viasurvey.org

MEDITATION

There are many ways to meditate but it is certainly very helpful to have guidance and instruction when you begin. One way to learn how to meditate might be with a local group or class that you can join. You will also find www.modernmeditator.com to be a really useful resource to introduce you to the basics of meditation and to various tools and resources that can help you with your ongoing meditation practice.

DISCOVER YOUR HAPPINESS LEVELS

There are several interesting questionnaires that can help you get an objective view of your levels of positive emotions and attributes at www.authentichappiness.org.

When you have a spare half hour, fill in some of the questionnaires and see what you can learn about yourself.

TRAININGS

The College of Wellbeing http://collegeofwellbeing.com Chris Johnstone who set up the College of Wellbeing also has a brilliant, short online Resilience training course available on Udemy. You can get this at 50% off by following his link on this page: http://collegeofwellbeing.com/personal-resilience-in-an-hour

The Penn University Resilience programs

http://ppc.sas.upenn.edu/services/penn-resilience-training

The Power of Happiness course – anentertaining 10-day online video course that guides you to greater happiness in a fun and thought provoking way. Presented by Vanessa van Edwards, the behavioral investigator who created the Science of People research organization. (Up to date information can be found on the Choosing Happier resources webpage www.choosing-happier.com/recommended)

HAPPINESS ORGANIZATIONS

Action for Happiness

Project Happiness

The Happiness Alliance

THE WORLD HAPPINESS INDEXES

The World Happiness Report

http://worldhappiness.report/

The Happy Planet Index

http://happyplanetindex.org/

POSITIVE MEDIA SOURCES

www.positive.news

www.constructivejournalism.com

INTERNATIONAL DAY OF HAPPINESS

http://www.happinessday.org/

http://www.dayofhappiness.net/#join

INTERNATIONAL POSITIVE ATTRIBUTE DAYS

These are days where kindness, compassion, gratitude, forgiveness, acceptance, smiling and laughter are being acknowledged and celebrated on an international level. You might like to mark these in your calendar as a way to have a fun and potentially social way of being focused on these great qualities with others.

The International Day of Acceptance on 20th January

Random Acts of Kindness Day 17th February (a whole week of random kind acts are encouraged around this date.)

International Day of Happiness 20th March (see below for more information)

World Laughter Day on the first Sunday of May

Character Strengths Day – September (dates vary)

World Gratitude Day on 21st September

The International Forgiveness Day in August (dates vary)

World Smile Day on the first Friday of October

World Kindness Day every 13th November

World Compassion Day every 28th November

RECOMMENDED BOOKS

A much more extensive and inspiring reading list that is being constantly updated can be found here:

http://www.choosing-happier.com/recommended

"The Art of Happiness" by the Dalai Lama and Howard Cutler

"The Book of Joy" by the Dalai Lama and Archbishop Desmond Tutu

"Learned Optimism" by Martin Seligman

"The Happiness Advantage" by Shawn Achor

"Flow: The Psychology of Optimal Experience" by Mihaly Csikszenmihalyi

"The How of Happiness: A Practical Guide to Getting the Life You Want" by Sonja Lyubomirsky

"Active Hope – how to face the mess that we are in without going crazy" by Chris Johnstone

"Find your Power – a toolkit for resilience and positive change" by Chris Johnstone

"The Resiliency Advantage – master change, thrive under pressure and bounce back from setbacks" by Al Siebert

INSPIRATIONAL STORIES OF RESILIENCE

"Endurance: Shackleton's incredible voyage to the Antarctic" by Alfred Lansing

CLUTTER CLEARING

"Spark Joy – an illustrated masterclass on the art of organizing and tidying up" by Marie Kondo

SLEEP SUPPORT

"Take a Nap" by Sara Mednick and Mark Ehrman

"Sleep Smarter" by Shawn Stevenson

INSPIRATIONAL AND SELF HELP

"A New Earth" and "The Power of Now" by Eckhart Tolle

"Jaguar in the Body, Butterfly in the Heart" by Ya'acov Darling Khan

"Movement Medicine" by Susannah and Ya'acov Darling Khan

"Be the Change" by Trenna Cormack

"Man's Search for Meaning" by Viktor E. Frankl

"The Biology of Belief" by Bruce Lipton

"Molecules of Emotion" by Candace Pert

READER BONUS MATERIALS REMINDER

I hope that you have really enjoyed reading this book and I am excited that you have embarked on this amazing journey to live more happily.

To support you in your desire to be happier I have created several tools and resources for you to download. These include printable tracking sheets, reminder cards, pay it forwards cards, MP3 meditations, etc. They will make your journey to increasing happiness easier, more effective, fun and enjoyable and they are all FREE.

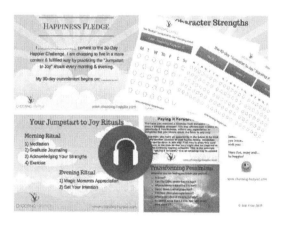

I have also created the "My Happiness Journal" which is a workbook that has been designed to be used in conjunction with this book. As you already have Choosing Happier, the book, you will get a 30% off discount code for the journal.

I will be creating even more useful aids to support you in living a more joy-full life and will inform you in the future as and when this toolbox increases! To access these tools and to get your discount code, just follow the link below.

http://www.choosing-happier.com/reader-bonuses

ACKNOWLEDGEMENTS

During my journey of finding clarity and a workable and effective path to happiness for myself, I used all of the exercises and practices that you will have learned about in this book. When I was doing the *honoring my influencers* exercise for the first time I remembered a teacher of mine from Kilburn Polytechnic College, in London, who I had not thought about for decades. Arnie Kurtz, who was Canadian by birth, taught something called Liberal Studies. This class was extra curriculum and an option that was purely designed to encourage us to look at our unquestioned beliefs and prejudices and to inspire us to become better people. I realized that Arnie had had a really important impact on the direction that I have taken in my life and so I wrote him a letter and attempted to discover where he lived now. Sadly, he passed away a few years ago and I was unable to express my appreciation directly to him. For that reason, I wanted to acknowledge what a wonderful and wise being he was here. I would also like to encourage you to do this exercise with the important people in your life before you miss that opportunity to tell them too.

Beyond Arnie, there have been so many people in my life who have positively impacted me and to whom I am truly grateful but I will not waste your precious time by writing a long meandering list of names that mean nothing to you. The ones that really stand out for me I have written letters to or will write letters to in the future.

There are many people who have been really supportive of my process of getting my thoughts and understandings down on paper. People who were particularly encouraging and helpful are Ellie, Lou, and Midi. Likewise, I am grateful to Volker Kaczinski for generously giving me permission to use his beautiful music as the background to the meditation and visualization recordings that I made for the happiness toolkit. Thanks also to Bruce Lipton Ph.D. for sharing his insight into how genes work and clarifying the fact that they are not responsible for nearly as many illnesses and states of being as people would like to blame them for!

On a practical level, I must offer a thank you to Ryan Eliason for the excellent productivity and focusing tips that have enabled me to actually complete this book on time in a relatively stress-free way. I would also like to appreciate Hal Elrod for his suggestions about how to create a movement to have a bigger impact and for inspiring me to start my days at 5 a.m.!

To all the other teachers and wonderful beings that I have had the privilege of meeting and being impacted by, I would also like to say thank you.

ABOUT THE AUTHOR

Jem **Friar** is a Health Coach, Life Coach, Happiness Coach, Naturopathic Consultant and the original Personal Detox Coach. He has trained in many forms of bodywork, yoga instruction and meditation. He presently lives near Dartmoor, in Devon, UK, where he is able to enjoy the luscious, green, rolling hills and a slower pace of country life.

Jem has a unique and fascinating perspective on life due to having spent 14 years living and working in over 50 countries around the world. He has also spent over 25 years working directly with individuals and groups as an alternative therapist and coach, supporting them to live in a more balanced, healthy and happy way. He has combined his wealth of experience with insights and practices from ancient traditions and modern science to lay out an easy to follow formula that will allow anyone to raise their happiness levels.

Apart from his focus on self-growth and healing work on the individual level, Jem is passionate about humanity's need to evolve and have a more benign impact on each other and our planet's biosphere. To this end, he created the "Happier Planet Mission Statement" which lies behind everything that he now does.

To inspire and enable people to live more content and happy lives so that we all express and experience a greater level of kindness, care and con-

sciousness. In this way, humanity as a whole will be able to thrive in an environmentally sustainable, benevolent, socially just and peaceful way on planet Earth.

When not writing, Jem is either coaching individuals and groups online or running detox retreats. His coaching is either focused on supporting people to improve their health and well-being or to live more happily and in alignment with their purpose. He is particularly passionate about coaching anyone working in the field of creating positive planetary change i.e. with change makers who are attempting to make this world a better place.

COACHING WITH JEM

If you are interested to learn more about Jem's happiness and true purpose coaching for individuals or groups go to:

http://www.choosing-happier.com/happiness-coaching

You can also learn more about Jem's detox and health coaching at
www.personaldetoxcoach.com

OTHER BOOKS BY JEM FRIAR

MY HAPPINESS JOURNAL

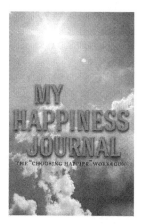

You will find this journal to be incredibly useful if used in conjunction with reading this book. I designed it to support you in becoming happier and more productive by applying the simplest and most effective techniques that I have suggested, on a daily basis. Doing at least 2 or 3 of the simple practices from this book each day will make a massive difference to your life.

Using a happiness journal is your foundational tool. You will find it to be really supportive and it will keep you focused on and inspired to do these simple exercises daily.

Readers of this book can buy it at a discounted rate, when you request your free Happiness Toolkit. Details are on the next page.

THE GRATITUDE ATTITUDE
– The First "How To Be Happy" Key

This is a short e-book about gratitude that was written in celebration of the International Day of Happiness. It introduces people to the realization that anyone can learn and choose to be happier by presenting some simple gratitude and appreciation exercises that readers can use to experience positive changes in their lives straight away.

It is being distributed for free as a means to spread happiness in the world.

You can find it at: www.books2read.com/gratitudeattitude

THE HEART MEDITATION
– a meditation to change your world

This is a short kindle book that focuses on a very beautiful meditation that is designed to help you to live in a more heart-centered way.

You can get it at www.bookstoread.com/heartmeditation

It is also possible to buy a recorded 35 minute version of the actual meditation set to music on CD.

This can be bought directly here:

http://www.choosing-happier.com/heart-med

If you are interested in learning more about meditation then you will find www.modernmeditator.com very useful.

DREAM JOURNALS

If you are interested in or fascinated by dreams then you will find these two dream journals really helpful. The Dream Journal is for anyone who likes to keep a record of their normal dreams. The Lucid Dream Journal has been designed to help people who are interested in lucid dreaming to access this heightened dream state more easily and effectively.

MY DREAM JOURNAL
– a book for recording the bizarre and beautiful world of my dreams.

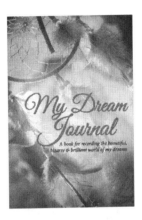

This beautiful journal has been designed to inspire the easy recording of one's dreams. The dream catcher theme of the cover is reflected in images found inside the book too. This journal is great for anyone who loves to keep a record of their night-time dream adventures.

This dream journal can be found at www.JournalEasy.com.

MY LUCID DREAM JOURNAL

– an ongoing record of my adventures and explorations into the world of Lucid Dreaming.

The Lucid Dream Journal has been written and designed in a way that will support anyone who is attempting to explore the incredible world of Lucid Dreaming. It is filled with practices that can help increase the possibility of, as well as heighten, the experience of lucid dreaming.

Apart from the main section being for recording dreams and lucid dreams, there are also sections for recording dream plans, dream signs, reality checks and lucid dream resources. The introduction clearly explains how to use the journal to best effect. This is a fantastic aid to the practice of lucid dreaming.

This dream journal can be found at www.JournalEasy.com.

THE JUICE HABIT MADE EASY – with tips, tricks and healthy fruit and vegetable recipes.

(Available as a printed book and as an e-book.)

This is a fantastic book to inspire, encourage and help you to juice regularly. There are so many benefits that come from having fresh juices but many people struggle with actually making their own juices. This book is packed with great tips, ideas and tricks that will help you to adopt the juicing habit and become a "Juicer." It also has some great mixed fruit and vegetable juice recipes for you to try.

"Highly recommended for anyone who seriously wants to have more juice in their life!"

The Personal Detox Coach's Simple Guides to Healthy Living Series – this series of easy guides to healthier living is being continually added to. More information and the latest books in the series by Jem can be found at:

http://www.personaldetoxcoach.com/books-cds

"A quiet secluded life in the country with the possibility of being useful to people to whom it is easy to do good and who are not accustomed to have it done to them; then work which one hopes may be of some use; then rest, nature, books, music, love for one's neighbor — such is my idea of happiness." — Leo Tolstoy

Mine too...

Made in the USA
San Bernardino, CA
07 June 2017